D0023654

READING LATIN EPITAPHS

This book is aimed at all who would like to be able to read Latin epitaphs in churches, but whose knowledge of the language may be sketchy.

The introduction explains the conventions involved in lettering, abbreviations, Latinized personal names, and stock phrases. It is followed by a very brief Latin grammar and notes on Roman numerals and dates. At the back of the book there is a word-list containing all those words found in the inscriptions, with numbered references, plus a selection of words which are commonly found in inscriptions elsewhere.

By bringing together these resources, the author equips the reader with the tools and confidence to tackle other epitaphs beyond the pages of this book and further afield.

John Parker is a retired teacher and has published three other books: *Crossnumbers* (1993), *The Platonic Solids* (2002) and *Ad Hoc, Ad Lib, Ad Nauseam* (2008). He also contributes to *Ad Familiares*, the journal of 'Friends of the Classics', which aims to disseminate the classics to the wider population.

READING LATIN EPITAPHS

A Handbook for Beginners
selected from West Country churches

NEW EDITION

John Parker

— The —
EXETER
PRESS

First published by Cressar Publications, Cornwall
in 1999, second edition 2000

This new edition first published in 2008 by
The Exeter Press Ltd
Reed Hall, Streatham Drive
Exeter EX4 4QR
UK
www.exeterpress.co.uk

© John H.D. Parker 2008

The right of John H.D. Parker to be identified as author of this
work has been asserted by him in accordance with
the Copyright, Designs and Patents Acts 1988.

British Library Cataloguing in Publication Data
A catalogue record for this book is available
from the British Library.

ISBN 978 1 905816 03 3

Printed in Great Britain by Booksprint

CONTENTS

THE 52 EPITAPHS

Introduction.

When we look at the walls of Britain's parish churches and cathedrals, we see that they are hung with memorials to the illustrious dead who once worshipped in those places, and who now lie buried in their vaults. Some of the dead were of noble birth, others were local gentry, a few were humble priests, but their memorials have always had a single purpose, to ensure that their names live for evermore. Many of those commemorated died suddenly or tragically or at an early age, and their epitaphs reflect the grief and deep sorrow of those they left behind. Reading these epitaphs today we can share in this sorrow, and it is very meet and right that we so do.

However, many of these epitaphs are written in Latin, and with so little Latin taught in schools nowadays, fewer and fewer people are able to read them. To me this seems a shame, and I have put this book together in the hope that it may help those with little or no knowledge of Latin to make some sense of the inscriptions they find on the walls of their local churches.

A word of warning. Latin is not an easy language to master, and this book can do little more than offer a helping hand along a road which at times can be extremely stony. I have given below the briefest possible account of the grammar of Latin, but the serious investigator sooner or later needs to be able to consult a standard book of Latin grammar, as well as a good dictionary. Suggestions for such books also appear below.

This word of warning having been given, a word of encouragement must be added. Most of the epitaphs in this selection, and indeed most of those found in churches, are written in relatively simple Latin. Furthermore the majority of epitaphs contain a number of stock phrases, and a recognition of such phrases can afford a valuable entry into the task of translating the whole inscription. In fact it is quite possible to construct a complete epitaph just by using these stock formulæ, as the following fictional example shows.

H. S. E. (Hic Sepultus est)   in spe resurrectionis
Here is buried   in hope of resurrection

Quicquid mortale fuit   Eduardi Benson A.M.
Whatever was mortal   of Edward Benson M.A.

Hujus ecclesiæ rectoris   per triginta annos
Rector of this church   for thirty years

Filii natu maximi   Gulielmi Benson
Eldest son   of William Benson

De Pirton   in comitatu Vigorniensi   Armiger
Of Pirton   in the county of Worcestershire   Esquire

Qui diem supremum obiit   sexto die Martii
Who died   on the sixth day of March

Anno Salutis MDCCXLIV   ætatis suæ LXVIII
A.D. 1744,   aged 68

Necnon Alicia   uxor carissima
Also Alice   the dearly beloved wife

Ipsius Eduardi supradicti
Of the above-named self-same Edward

Et filia natu secunda   et cohæres
And second daughter   and co-heir

Johannis Cole   de Clystæ Sanctæ Mariæ
Of John Cole   of Clyst St. Mary

In agro Devoniæ   Armigeri
In the county of Devon,   Esquire

Quæ morti occubuit   duodevicesimo die Februarii
Who succumbed to death   on the 18th day of February

Anno Domini MDCCXXXIII   ætatis suæ XLIX
A.D. 1733,   aged 49

Requiescant in pace
May they rest in peace.

Petrus filius prædicti unicus superstes
Peter the only surviving son of the above-mentioned

Moerens   hoc monumentum   in pietate
In his grief   this monument   in filial affection

Poni curavit
Caused to be placed.

The 52 epitaphs. Each of these is preceded by the name of the church in which the memorial is to be found. Most of these churches are in Devon and in neighbouring counties; some no longer exist, having been destroyed in the air raids on Exeter. Epitaphs included here from these churches have been copied from transcriptions made before the war by earlier researchers. Each epitaph is followed by a translation, and by a number of notes. These notes are progressive; once a particular feature of an epitaph has been commented on, subsequent appearances of the same feature are usually passed over without comment. Reference numbers in the word list at the end of the book show in which epitaph the relevant comment has been made, so the reader of **37** who is perhaps puzzled by the word ARMIG is referred by the word list to relevant notes in **2** and **10**.

The epitaphs are arranged approximately in order of difficulty. The earlier ones are easier to read, through being grammatically a little less complicated than the later ones. I have tried to reproduce them fairly faithfully, keeping the line pattern of the originals and the word breaks where these occur (see **41** for an extreme example). Most epitaphs were cut into stone by stonemasons, although some earlier ones were realised in paint or in gold leaf on wood. Most were presented in rectangular frames, although a few, such as those in **17**, **33** and **46**, were inscribed in circular or oval frames, and this shows in the line pattern. Some were inscribed in capitals throughout, others in both upper and lower case letters. Some contain errors of spelling, usually the fault of the mason who misread the handwritten copy given him by the composer of the inscription. It must be remembered that the mason did not normally know Latin and was a mere copyist, and that mistakes made in stone are not easily put right. Examples are not infrequently found however of errors which have been corrected in the stone; in the original of **14** *virgo* has been corrected from *vergo* and *annorum* from *annoram*. It is also easy to make mistakes in transcription which go unnoticed even after several checks, so that I apologise in advance for any which I myself may have perpetrated.

Some inscriptions often look somewhat alien in that they seem to contain too many v's. In Classical Latin, especially in inscriptions carved in stone, "u" was almost invariably shown as "v", and many inscriptions in our churches are faithful to this tradition. On the other hand, although there was no "j" in Classical Latin (this developed later as a long "i"), many inscriptions have j's in place of some i's. So we meet HVJVS for *huius* ("of this") and IVLIJ for *Iulii* ("of July") and QVVM ("when") for *quum*. However, the composer of **52** travelled in the reverse direction when he wrote *niuei* for *nivei* and *maritauit* for *maritavit*!

Abbreviations. Considerations of space, of cost, and, especially when memorials were carved in stone, of time and effort, meant that words were often abbreviated. Many abbreviations were conventional, so that for instance *arm* appears for *armiger* almost as often as we write "Esq." as an abbreviation of "Esquire". In transcribing the epitaphs I have retained the abbreviations, with an explanatory note where I have judged this to be necessary.

One particular class of abbreviation was adopted originally by scribes and copyists and was widely used in mediæval manuscript books and in handwritten legal documents. The Latin ending -*um* was shortened to -*u* with a flourish or line drawn over it to indicate that an "m" was missing. (We still use exactly the same kind of abbreviation when we write "@" for "at".) The saving in time could not have been great but it presumably helped. The practice was carried over into written or carved memorials, so that in **52** we read the words *du, nimiu, futuru*, standing for *dum, nimium, futurum*, respectively. Here the stratagem reduces the length of the line just sufficiently to allow it to fit the space available.

This practice was extended to indicate omissions generally, so that we find *Johes* for *Johannes*, *ultim* for *ultimo*, *Domi* for *Domini*. Especially we find a double -nn- reduced to a single -ñ-, as in *año* for *anno*. The sign for this abbreviation is known generally by its Spanish name of *tilde*, and was in fact used originally in Spanish to indicate a missing -n- at a time when a double -nn- was used to express the sound "ny". For instance "sennor", pronounced "senyor", was shortened to "señor". This spelling soon became standard, and the tilde has now become a fixed feature of Spanish orthography.

Latin has a number of words for "and" - *et, ac, atque* - and it also has a suffix, -*que*. For instance in **5** we read *rectoris filiique*, meaning "rector and son". This -*que* is often reduced to -*q*, with or without a small squiggle at its tail, so that in **46** *ejusq* is short for *ejusque*, "and his", while in **17** *totidemq* is short for *totidemque*, "and just as many". Note that in the English translation, the "and" moves to the front of the phrase. Note also that even when the -*que* is an integral part of a word, as in *quoque*, "also", it may still be abbreviated, so that we find *quoq* in **10**.

4

The epitaphs tell us a lot about those who composed them. On the whole they knew their Latin. Some were parish priests, others were scholars or educated members of the bereaved family. They had been to Oxford or Cambridge and had read the Classical authors, especially Horace and Virgil and Cicero, and echoes of these authors and allusions to their writings recur frequently in the more flowery epitaphs. The composers knew their grammar and their syntax. Occasionally they misspelt words, perhaps through normal forgetfulness, but misspellings (as against miscopyings) are very rare. Variant spellings do appear occasionally, perhaps as the result of changes in fashion. For example, the classical *mærens*, "mourning", frequently appears as *moerens*, possibly influenced by the English word. Again, although few explicit references are made in these epitaphs to the Latin Vulgate Bible or to Roman Catholic Latin liturgy, such spellings as *ejus* for *eius* which, as we can see in the Latin titles of the Psalms in the Book of Common Prayer, were standard in Church Latin, occur frequently in memorials.

The translations. I have tried to stick fairly closely to the literal sense of the Latin, so that the reader can connect each word or phrase of the translation to its Latin counterpart. For example the word *moerens* means "grieving" or "mourning", and generally I have used one of these words as a translation, although in the fictional example on page 2 I have instead used the phrase "in his grief". I believe either translation is acceptable. However one important point arises here. The composer of each epitaph could have chosen to write it in English, but for whatever reason he chose instead to write it in Latin. Although we can make a guess at what he might have said had he chosen to use English - at least as many epitaphs of the era were written in English as were written in Latin, so we know the kind of phraseology and vocabulary which were fashionable - the fact remains that he chose to write in Latin. Presumably Latin was better able to express what he wanted to say, so that any English translation can express his intentions only approximately. There are some stock equivalents in the two languages: "caused to be placed" appears in inscriptions as a parallel to *poni curavit*, and "a remarkable sweetness of nature" is to be found alongside *ingenii suavitas eximia*, but for many Latin phrases it is often virtually impossible to find an English rendering of comparable elegance and succinctness, and I have usually chosen to make do with a very pedestrian translation.

5

The Word List. One important fact will be obvious to readers when they consult the word list. Any word in Latin may have a number of different meanings in English, and this makes translation a matter of careful choice. Sometimes I have given three meanings in the word list to a word like *felix*, and have then used a fourth meaning in a translation. Even a dictionary of modest size will offer a further half-dozen meanings, so the translator is not starved of choice. Conversely the composer often had a wide choice of Latin words and phrases in which to express a single idea in English. The outstanding example is "died", which has its own euphemisms in any language: the epitaphs here offer *obiit, decessit, obdormivit, recessit, morti occubuit, morti succubuit*, and many others.

Names. Most of the place names which appear in the epitaphs are written in their English form - Stockley Pomeroy, Dulwich. A very few are written in their Latinised form - *Exonia* for Exeter, *Vigornia* for Worcester. In general, therefore, place names should cause little difficulty. Personal (Christian) names are more frequently Latinised, and a mention is made of some of these at the end of the word list. Some men's names were Latinised by the addition of Latin endings - *Robertus, Josephus*; others were written in the earlier forms from which the familiar forms were derived - *Johannes* (John), *Jacobus* (James), *Gulielmus* (William). Most are readily recognisable, and the same relatively few names appear over and over again. Names like *Baldewin* and *Rice* are rare.

Women's names are usually much more readily recognisable than those of the men. Winifred and Elizabeth are give Latin shape by the simple addition of -a; *Winifreda, Elizabetha*. Anne appears as *Anna*, Joan (or Joanna) as *Johanna*, Mary as *Maria*. I have generally written these names in their modern form, unless good reason exists for doing otherwise. For instance independent sources tell us that Baldewin Fulford's mother (**23**) was Anna-Maria (Adams) rather than Anne-Mary, and that John Fiennes' mother (**52**) was Susannah (Hobbes) rather than Susanna.

The Grammar of Latin. There is unfortunately no escaping the need to know a good deal about the grammar of Latin if one is to make a reasonable attempt at translating even the simplest of Latin epitaphs. The limited importance attached in Latin to word-order means that if one is to make any sense of an inscription, one may have to establish grammatical links between words which are more or less widely separated. For example in **11** it is essential to know enough grammar to link *tutissimas* with *cunas* in the next line down, and to link *invenit* with *qui* appearing earlier two lines up. The next few pages attempt to give a brief outline of some of the basic grammar of Latin, and the notes for the 52 epitaphs seek to explain new points of grammar as they arise. However, the reader will soon need to be able to refer to a much fuller Latin grammar, such as Kennedy's Shorter Latin Primer (Longman), and to have access to a good dictionary, such as Cassell's Latin Dictionary, or to Lewis and Short's comprehensive dictionary, available in many reference libraries. A useful book, which contains much of the grammar needed, is "Teach Yourself Beginner's Latin" but there is a choice of others on the market.

After the outline of basic grammar we take a glance at dates and at the Roman calendar, with its Calends, Ides and Nones, used in some epitaphs. At the end of the central section containing the 52 epitaphs, as has already been mentioned, there is a word list. This contains, with few exceptions, all the words found in the epitaphs, together with a number of others which the reader may find useful to know when trying to translate epitaphs from other sources.

Acknowledgements

At this point it would normally be appropriate to thank the various church authorities concerned for their permission to use the epitaphs printed in this book. It would seem, however, that such permission is not needed, and so all I can do is to thank the Bishops of Truro and of Exeter for their help and for the interest they have shown in the project.

I am deeply grateful to the late Mr. Desmond Lisle Clements and to Dr. Peter Jones for disentangling for me a few of the knottier points of grammar and interpretation. No doubt I should have consulted them more often: it is to be understood that any errors and other shortcomings in this book are my own unaided efforts.

I must also thank Mr. Richard Bass and Dr. Shelagh Gregory for pointing out certain errors in the first two editions of this book. These errors have now been corrected. I am also deeply indebted to Dr. Neil Cheshire and to Mr. Geoffrey Allibone for suggesting a number of improvements to the translations. These improvements appear in the current edition.

"The language of the country of which a learned man was a native is not the language fit for his epitaph, which should be in ancient and permanent language". Dr. Samuel Johnson.

.

A (Very) Brief Latin Grammar

Word Order and Word Endings.

If we make the simple statement in English "Anne loves John", then we have a sentence containing two nouns and a verb. The verb is "loves"; the subject of the verb is "Anne", and "John" is the object, not just of Anne's affections, but of the verb as well.

If we put this same sentence word for word into Latin, it becomes "Anna amat Johannem", with "Anna" the subject, "amat" the verb, and "Johannem" the object. Straightaway we meet some of the features in which Latin differs from English. For a start the English sentence "John loves Anne" would mean something quite different from "Anne loves John", since the meaning of a sentence in English is very much determined by the order in which the words occur. However the Latin "Johannem amat Anna" means exactly the same as "Anna amat Johannem", with perhaps a slight change of emphasis. This is because the ending "-a" of "Ann-a" and the ending "-em" of "Johann-em" are enough to tell us exactly what part the two words play in the sentence, no matter whereabouts they are in it. To say "John loves Anne" in Latin we have to change the word endings and write "Johannes amat Annam", where "Johannes" is the new subject and "Annam" is the new object. We have altered the functions of the two words not by altering the order in which they come, but by altering their form.

[Note that we have something similar in the English sentences, "She loves him" and "He loves her", although only if we use personal pronouns, which in English still have different forms for subject and object. Since the form of the pronoun shows what its function is in the sentence, the word order in either sentence can be altered slightly without destroying the meaning entirely - "Him she loves", "Loves he her", - but only within very narrow limits.]

Word Endings.

The endings of the (Latin) words "Anna", "Annam", "Johannes" and "Johannem" are of the utmost importance and cannot be ignored. Each word can be split into two parts, the *stem* or *root*, and the ending: "Ann-a", "Johann-em," etc. The endings tell us what each word is doing in the sentence: "Ann-a" and "Johann-es" have *nominative* endings, telling us that here we have the *subject* of the sentence: "Ann-am" and "Johann-em" have *accusative* endings, telling us that here we have the *object* of the sentence. This means that we can combine the three words in any order we choose, including for example "Amat Johannem Anna" and "Johannem Anna amat", without losing the basic meaning of the sentence, although the emphasis may be changed slightly. No matter where it appears, "Anna" will be the subject of the sentence: "Johannem" will always be the object. [Latin in fact generally tends to place the verb at the end of the sentence, so "Anna Johannem amat" is, we may say, the preferred order.]

Nominative and *accusative* are examples of *cases*, helping to show the function of a noun in a sentence. Other cases are the *genitive*, the *dative* and the *ablative*, which are discussed below, and the *vocative* and *locative* which are referred to in the notes to the epitaphs. The vocative is used in addressing a person or object ("vocally"), while the locative indicates a place or "location".

Latin nouns are divided into classes or *declensions*, each with its more or less distinctive case endings. The (accusative) endings of the two words *Annam* and *Johannem* are different because the words have been assigned to different declensions. Sometimes the case ending indicates precisely to which declension the noun belongs - *Annam* for instance can only belong to the first declension - but often enough the same ending, such as *-em* or *-i*, is shared by cases from two or more different declensions.

Each noun also has a *gender* assigned to it, masculine or feminine or neuter. The dictionary indicates what this gender is, and a writer will generally need to know the gender of any noun he uses since qualifying adjectives must *agree* with their nouns, that is, they must have the correct ending both for case and for gender (as well as for *number*, singular or plural).

Nouns: *The Nominative Case* The word "nominative" derives from the Latin *nomen, nominis*, "a name", and the nominative case gives a name to whatever subject we are talking about. The nominative (singular) ending of nouns of the "first declension" is *-a*. Examples include *anima*, "soul"; *filia*, "daughter"; and *benevolentia*, "benevolence" (and *Anna*, "Anne"). Most of these words are feminine in gender, and qualifying adjectives must agree with them and be feminine in form. (*Vide infra*, "see below".)

[Note: for economy of wording the word "singular" will generally be omitted in the account which follows, so that, for example, "nominative" must be understood to mean "nominative *singular*", and so also for the other cases. If *plural* endings are under consideration, this will be made clear.]

Most of the nouns of the "second declension" are masculine in gender, and have the nominative ending -*us*. Examples include *amicus*, "friend"; *annus*, "year"; *filius*, "son"; and *Ricardus*, "Richard". Some second declension nouns however are neuter, and their nominative ending is -*um*. Examples include *ærarium*, "treasury"; *argumentum*, "debate"; and *balneum*, "bath". A few second declension masculine nouns end in the nominative in -*er* only, but otherwise behave as if they ended in -*erus*. Most, but not all, of these nouns represent persons. Examples are *puer*, "boy"; *armiger*, "esquire"; and *liber*, "book".

For nouns of the "third declension", of which there are very many, the nominative endings vary, and it is usually impossible to tell from its nominative form whether a particular noun is masculine, feminine or neuter. Examples include *ætas*, "age"; *gens*, "clan" (both feminine); *mercator*, "merchant"; *flos,* "flower"; *frater*, "brother" (all masculine): and *cadaver*, "corpse" and *corpus*, (confusingly *not* second declension!), "body" (both neuter). Some nouns have the ending -*is* which marks them as being third declension: examples include *civis*, "citizen"; *iuvenis*, "young man"; and *mensis*, "month".

Nouns of the "fourth declension" have nominatives ending in -*us* or (for neuter nouns) in -*u*. Examples include *comitatus*, "county"; *fructus*, "fruit", (both masculine); *manus*, "hand" and, in the plural only, *Idus*, "Ides" (both feminine).

"Fifth declension" nouns end in -*es* in the nominative, and are nearly all feminine. Examples are *dies*, "day" (sometimes masculine, especially in dates); *fides*, "faith"; and *spes*, "hope".

Nouns: *The Accusative Case*. This has nothing to do with accusing, but a lot to do with causing. The subject of the verb causes something to happen: that something happens to the object of the verb, which is normally in the accusative case. All accusative singular nouns of any declension, with the exception of some neuter nouns, end in -*am* or -*em* or -*um*. The accusative of neuter nouns is the same as the nominative: the accusative singular of *balneum* is *balneum*, while the accusative singular of *cadaver* is simply *cadaver*.

The accusative is used not only for the object of a verb but also after certain prepositions, such as *ante*, "before"; *erga,* "towards"; *in*, "into";

iuxta, "next to"; *per*, "through"; and *post*, "after". Examples are *ante meridiem*, "before mid-day" (our *a.m.*); and *post mortem*, "after death".

Nouns: *The Genitive Case* This should perhaps more properly be the "generic" case, since it links a noun to a *genus* or family. It also denotes possession. "Edward's wife " or "the wife of Edward" is *coniux Eduardi*, where *Eduardi* is the genitive of *Eduardus*. Nouns of the first declension have genitives in *-æ*; those of the second and fifth declension have genitives in *-i*; those of the third declension have genitives in *-is*; while those of the fourth declension have genitives in *-us*.

E.g.:	1st	filiæ	of a daughter
	2nd	filii	of a son
	3rd	ætatis	of age
	4th	comitatus	of a county
	5th	fidei	of faith

Nouns: *The Dative Case*. This is used relatively infrequently, usually when something is given to or dedicated to something. The term comes from the word *datum*, "given". The endings for the various declensions can be found in any grammar book.

Nouns: *The Ablative Case* This case is found much more frequently than the dative. The term comes from the word *ablatum*, "taken from". Without a preposition it can mean (among other things) "by" or "with" or "from" or "in" or "on", so that *anno* can mean "in the year" and *morte* can mean "by death". However the ablative is also used after certain prepositions, such as *a*, "from"; *cum*, "with"; *e* or *ex*, "out of"; *in*, "in"; and *pro*, "on behalf of". The endings for the various declensions are as follows:

	1st	-a, often written as -â
	2nd	-o
	3rd	-e, with a few exceptions in -i
	4th	-u, with one exception, *domo* ("out of the house")
	5th	-e

E.g.:	1st	causâ	for the sake of
	2nd	morbo	through illness
	3rd	sorte	in rank
	4th	natu	by birth
	5th	die	on the day

More about endings.

We can now expand the original sentence a little. *Anna filia Ricardi Jones Armigeri amat Johannem filium Gulielmi Smith, Mercatoris, magno cum amore*. "Anne, daughter of Richard Jones, Esquire, loves John, son of William Smith, merchant, with great affection". The basic sentence is still there: *Anna amat Johannem*, but we now know more about Anne and John. *Anna* is the daughter, *filia*, of Richard Jones. *Filia* is "in apposition to" *Anna* - they are both the same person, Anne, and they are both in the same case, nominative, and share the same ending -*a*. Likewise *filium* is in apposition to *Johannem*, and although their endings -*um* and -*em* are different (second and third declensions respectively), each is the appropriate accusative ending for its own word, whose nominative form is respectively *filius* and *Johannes*.

Ricardi and *Gulielmi* - "of Richard" (*Ricardus*), "of William" (*Gulielmus*) - both have a genitive ending -*i*. Here the genitive case expresses the idea of possession or ownership. We see the same genitive ending -*i* in *Armigeri*, which is in apposition to *Ricardi*, and so has to be genitive as well. *Mercatoris* is the genitive of *Mercator* and is in apposition to *Gulielmi*, but the ending here is -*is* and not -*i* because *Mercator* and *Gulielmus* belong to different declensions, third and second respectively, each with its own distinctive case endings.

The phrase *magno cum amore* illustrates another special feature of Latin. Words which in English normally (and seemingly naturally) occur side by side (*magno...amore,* "great affection") are often separated in Latin as a matter simply of style. *Cum* is a preposition "governing" *amore* which is the ablative of *amor*, as the ending -*e* shows. The adjective *magno* is attached to *amore* - in grammatical language *magno* "qualifies" *amore* - and is for this reason also in the ablative case, as the ending -*o* shows. Note that *amor* is masculine: *magno* is the ablative of *magnus*, "great", the nominative *masculine* singular form of the adjective. If we were to replace *amor* with *caritas*, another word for "love" (but feminine, not masculine*)*, then the phrase would become *magna cum caritate*, where *caritate* is the ablative of *caritas* and *magna* is the ablative *feminine* singular of *magna*, the nominative *feminine* singular of the adjective.

[It would seem to follow from the above that *magna* (nominative) and *magna* (ablative) are the same word. In ancient Rome, however, the two words differed in speech, with the nominative *magna* ending in a short "a", and the ablative *magna* ending in a long "a". In the original epitaphs it is quite common to find this long "a" marked with a circumflex accent, as "â", so our new phrase would read "magnâ cum caritate". *Vide supra*, ("see above"), under "Nouns: *The Ablative Case*".]

We can summarise the facts we have amassed so far in a table (opposite), where we have filled in any gaps, including the plurals of each noun. These plural forms are also usually explained individually whenever they occur in a particular epitaph, and can always be found displayed in the grammar books.

[Note: *Armiger* takes the same endings as *filius*; *mercator* behaves like *amor*.]

Adjectives

We have already mentioned that adjectives must agree in gender, case and number (i.e. singular or plural) with the nouns they qualify. For example *homines boni*, "good men", is the (masculine) nominative plural of *homo bonus*, and *insigni patientiâ*, "by a remarkable patience", is the (feminine) ablative singular of *insignis patientia*. [Note that *boni* on its own can mean "good men". Latin sometimes uses adjectives in place of nouns just as English does, for example, in the claim that "none but the brave deserves the fair".]

Adjectives also have *comparative* and *superlative* forms, both in English and in Latin: "good, better, best" are paralleled by *bonus, melior, optimus*, and "large, larger, largest" are paralleled by *magnus, maior, maximus*. These examples however are irregular; the regular forms can be seen in *carus, carior, carissimus*, "dear, dearer, dearest", and in *felix, felicior, felicissimus*, "joyous, more joyous, most joyous" (the stem of *felix* being *felic-*). These comparatives and superlatives can be declined as ordinary adjectives to agree with the nouns they qualify.

One use of the superlative in Latin is to express the notion of "very" or "extremely". So *vir clarissimus*, "most distinguished man", can be translated as "highly distinguished man", and *uxor amatissima* can be translated as "dearly loved wife". [Note that *amatissima* is a superlative form of *amatus*, which is a past participle (*vide infra*), and which behaves here like an adjective.]

Nouns: Case Endings

	1st Declension	2nd Declension	3rd Declension	4th Declension	5th Declension
Singular					
Nominative	filia	filius	amor	manus	dies
Accusative	filiam	filium	amorem	manum	diem
Genitive	filiæ	filii	amoris	manus	diei
Dative	filiæ	filio	amori	manui	diei
Ablative	filia	filio	amore	manu	die
Plural					
Nominative	filiæ	filii	amores	manus	dies
Accusative	filias	filios	amores	manus	dies
Genitive	filiarum	filiorum	amorum	manuum	dierum
Dative	filiis	filiis	amoribus	manibus	diebus
Ablative	filiis	filiis	amoribus	manibus	diebus

Adverbs

Some adverbs are derived from adjectives. There are two ways in which this may happen. If the adjective behaves like nouns of the second declension and so ends in -us, etc., the ending -e is added to the stem, as in *eximi-e*, "remarkably", from *eximi-us*, "remarkable". If the adjective behaves like nouns of the third declension, then the ending -iter is added to the stem, as in *fidel-iter* "faithfully", from *fidel-is*, "faithful", and *felic-iter*, "successfully", from *felix*, "successful" (stem *felic-* as if the nominative were *felic-s*). Details of exceptions to these rules are to be found in the grammar books. Other adverbs such as *bene, fere, nunc*, are independent, though not a few are considered to have been derived originally from adjectives.

Verbs

Latin verbs, like Latin nouns, are made up of stems and endings, and are divided into four classes known as "conjugations". Verb endings vary with the conjugation and also with person (first, second, third), with number (singular, plural), with tense (present, future, etc.), with voice (active, passive), and with mood (indicative, subjunctive), but only a few points need be made here. A full explanation of each verb is normally given in the notes whenever it first appears in the epitaphs, and as usual, full details can be found in the grammar books.

In the table opposite we show the forms taken by two verbs, *amo* and *sum*, in two of their tenses, present and perfect, noting that the endings are related to the subject of the verb and so tell us *who* is doing whatever we are talking about.

Amo, "I love", has the stem "am-" and the ending "-o". "-O" is the ending of the first person singular present active indicative of all verbs except some irregular verbs, and *deponent* verbs, which are explained below. As is mentioned in the introduction to the word list, this is the form under which the verb is listed in the dictionary.

The third person singular present verb *amat* can be divided into three parts: the stem "am-", and a composite ending "-a-t". The "-a-" has been called the "key" vowel and indicates here that the verb is a "first conjugation" verb. The "-t" is the usual ending for any third person singular (active) verb. *Amat* can mean "he loves" or "she loves" or "it loves". The *infinitive* of the verb is *am-a-re*, "to love".

Verbs: Endings

Person	Tense	Present		Perfect	
1st Singular		Amo	I love	Amavi	I have loved
2nd Singular		Amas	You love	Amavisti	You have loved
3rd Singular		Amat	He/she/it loves	Amavit	He/she/it has loved
1st Plural		Amamus	We love	Amavimus	We have loved
2nd Plural		Amatis	You love	Amavistis	You have loved
3rd Plural		Amant	They love	Amaverunt	They have loved
1st Singular		Sum	I am	Fui	I have been/was
2nd Singular		Es	You are	Fuisti	You have been/were
3rd Singular		Est	He/she/it is	Fuit	He/she/it has been/was
1st Plural		Sumus	We are	Fuimus	We have been/were
2nd Plural		Estis	You are	Fuistis	You have been/were
3rd Plural		Sunt	They are	Fuerunt	They have been/were

The third person singular *perfect* verb *amavit* can also be divided into three parts, *am-av-it*. The "-av-" indicates that the verb is of the first conjugation, and "amav-" can be regarded as the *perfect* stem of the verb. The "-it" is the usual ending for any third person singular perfect (active) verb and includes the "-t" (third person singular) ending mentioned above. The other endings, *-i, -isti, -imus*, etc., are regular perfect endings. Most verbs in the epitaphs ending in "-it" will be third person singular perfect verbs, although *-it* can also be a present tense ending. For example *vixit* (with stem *vix-*) is perfect and means "(he) lived", while *vivit* (stem *viv-*) is present and means "(he) lives". The perfect stem is usually different from the present stem. (Even *fugit*, "he flees" and *fugit*, "he fled", are distinguished in speech by the length of the vowel "u".) The dictionary entry for most verbs includes the first person perfect active indicative.

The verb *sum,* "I am", with infinitive *esse*, "to be", is irregular, with its parts being gathered from several different source verbs (cf. "am", "is", "are", was", in English). The perfect tense however has a stem "fu-" and regular endings. Other tenses of *esse*, as the grammar books will attest, have various stems but regular endings.

The present tense and the perfect tense are those most frequently found in epitaphs. The perfect tense is a past tense, used for actions which have been completed, whose aim has been achieved and *perfected*. For this reason *amavi* can be translated either as "I have loved" or simply as "I (once upon a time) loved"; while *fuerunt* is either "they have been" or "they (once) were". In **26** however we meet two verbs which come from another tense of *esse*, the *imperfect* tense: *eram*, "I used to be" and *erat*, "he used to be". This tense here posits a continuous state of existence, with no hint of a time limit.

Verbs from other conjugations have different "key vowels" but behave generally in much the same way as *amo*. For instance the fourth conjugation verb *invenio*, "I find", has a stem *inven-*, with the "key vowel" *-i-* and infinitive *inven-i-re*. The present tense is *invenio, invenis, invenit*, etc., while the perfect tense is *inveni, invenisti, invenit*, etc., with a long "e" to distinguish the perfect stem from the present stem. The third declension *pono, ponis, ponit*, etc., "I place", has no particular "key vowel": its infinitive is *ponere* and its perfect is *posui, posuisti, posuit*, etc. The second declension *teneo*, "I hold", has a key vowel *-e-*, an infinitive *tenere*, and a perfect *tenui, tenuisti*, etc.

Verbs - *Passive Voice*

The verbs we have been looking at so far are in the "active voice", a technical term which indicates that in, for example, the verb "I love", the subject, "I", is initiating the action. However, in the sentence "I am loved", someone else is doing the loving, while I am *passively* accepting that love. In "I am loved" the verb is in the "passive voice". In Latin "I love" is *amo;* "I am loved" is *amor.* "He loves" is *amat*; "he is loved" is *amatur.* "I have loved" is *amavi*; "I have been loved" is *amatus sum.* Full details will be found in the grammar books.

Verbs - *Deponent Verbs*

Some verbs are *passive* in form but *active* in meaning, and are known as *deponent* verbs. *Morior* looks as if it should be the passive of *morio*, "I die", but there is no such word as *morio*, and *morior* itself means "I die". *Testantur* looks as if it should be the passive of *testant* but it is in fact the third person plural present *active* of *testor*, "I bear witness", and means "they bear witness". Both *morior* and *testantur* are parts of *deponent* verbs.

Verbs - *Participles*

In the phrases "a loving mother", "a much-loved teddy-bear", "the dying moments", "a dead certainty", we have parts of verbs used as adjectives. "Loving" and "dying" are *present participles* of "love" and "die"; "loved" and "dead" are the respective *past participles* of the two verbs.

These participles exist also in Latin. The present participle of *amo*, "I love", is *amans*, "loving", while the present participle of *morior*, "I die", is *moriens*, "dying". These can be used as if they were adjectives behaving like nouns of the third declension; their respective genitive singular forms are *amantis* and *morientis*.

The past participle of *amo* is *amatus*, "loved", which is used to construct the passive voice - *amatus sum*, "I have been loved" (*vide supra*); the past participle of *morior* is *mortuus*, "dead". These can be used as if they were adjectives behaving like nouns of the first and second declensions, so that, for example, *amatus* has three nominative forms, *amatus, amata, amatum*, and two genitive forms, *amati, amatæ*. Like adjectives, these participles can be used on their own as nouns, so that *amans* may mean "a lover" and *mortuus* may mean "a dead man".

Verbs - *Gerundives*

These also behave like adjectives behaving in their turn like nouns of the first and second declensions. For example the gerundive *amandus*, meaning "to be loved", has a feminine nominative *amanda*, (whence the familiar girl's name). Gerundives often imply a lesser or greater degree of (moral) compulsion. They are linked to *gerunds* which behave like neuter nouns of the second declension and end in -*um* in the nominative. They give words and phrases familiar in English usage: a *memorandum* is something which has to be remembered; an *agenda* (plural of *agendum*) contains things which must be acted upon; a *referendum* lays out matters to be referred to the electorate; *corrigenda* are mistakes requiring correction; *nil desperandum* seeks to reassure us that nothing is to be despaired of.

Verbs - *The Subjunctive Mood*

So far we have looked only at verbs in their *indicative* mood, in which they *indicate* that something has happened or is happening. However when we talk about things which might or might not have happened, or which may happen but about whose happening there is some doubt, however slight, then the verb may well appear in the *subjunctive* mood. In English the subjunctive still survives in such phrases as "If I *were* you" and "Whether it *please* God to take him or not", and in the expression of wishes - "God *bless* you!", "Long *live* the Queen!". In Latin the subjunctive is shown by altering word endings: *requiescit in pace* (indicative) means "he rests in peace", while *requiescat in pace* (subjunctive) means "may he rest in peace". Again, full details will be found in the grammar books.

Pronouns

Just as English uses pronouns such as "I" and "you" and "it" and "who" to refer to persons or things, so Latin possesses its own similar pronouns. The grammar books will give full lists: a few observations are worth making here.

Personal pronouns met with in the epitaphs include *ego*, "I"; *me*, "me"; *tu*, "thou"; *te*, "thee", as well as forms of *is, ea, id*, "he, she, it". Particularly frequent is *eius* or *ejus*, the common genitive of *is, ea, id*, meaning "of him, of her, of it", i.e., "his, hers, its", used when referring to a person who is not the subject of the sentence.

Possessive pronouns are used when referring to a person who *is* the subject of a sentence. For "his, hers, its" the stem is *su-*: the nominative singular of the three genders is *suus, sua, suum*, and they agree with their nouns in case, number and gender - *filius suus*, "his (or her) son"; *liberi sui*, "her (or his) children"; *a patre suo*, "from her father"; *ætatis suæ*, "of his age".

Demonstrative pronouns draw attention to "this" or "that". "This" is expressed by forms of *hic, hæc, hoc*, while "that" is expressed by forms of *ille, illa, illud*. The common genitive of *hic*, etc., which is *huius* or *hujus*, occurs frequently - *huius ecclesiæ*, "of this church"; *huius oppidi*, "of this town".

Relative pronouns refer to "who" or "what" we are talking about, and are generally forms of *qui, quæ, quod*. The common genitive of these is *cuius*, "of whom, whose".

This account of Latin grammar is exceedingly brief and is no more than a beginning but it should just be enough to provide help on the way to understanding how simple epitaphs are put together.

Dates

Most dates on memorials translate as "on such-and-such a day of such-and-such a month in such-and-such a year", and so we can expect to see the *ablative* endings used for the days and years, and the *genitive* endings used for the months. So for someone who died on 6th November 1700 we would expect to read perhaps *obiit sexto (die)* [ablative] *(mensis) Novembris* [genitive] *anno* [ablative] 1700 - "he died on the sixth (day) of (the month of) November in the year 1700". [*Vide* also note on MDCXXXVIII° in **12**.]

The Latin names of the months of the year look quite familiar to us since we took the names of our own months from the Romans.

Here is a list of the months. The third column shows the *genitive* case, "of January", etc.

English	Latin	"of"
January	Januarius	Januarii
February	Februarius	Februarii
March	Martius	Martii
April	Aprilis	Aprilis
May	Maius	Maii
June	Junius	Junii
July	Julius	Julii
August	Augustus	Augusti
September	September	Septembris
October	October	Octobris
November	November	Novembris
December	December	Decembris

The numbers we need to recognise are the *ordinal* numbers: the third column shows the ablative case

first	primus	primo
second	secundus	secundo
third	tertius	tertio
fourth	quartus	quarto
fifth	quintus	quinto
sixth	sextus	sexto
seventh	septimus	septimo
eighth	octavus	octavo

ninth	nonus	nono
tenth	decimus	decimo
eleventh	undecimus	undecimo
twelfth	duodecimus	duodecimo
thirteenth	tertius decimus	tertio decimo
fourteenth	quartus decimus	quarto decimo
fifteenth	quintus decimus	quinto decimo
sixteenth	sextus decimus	sexto decimo
seventeenth	septimus decimus	septimo decimo
eighteenth	octavus decimus	octavo decimo
	duodevicesimus	duodevicesimo
nineteenth	nonus decimus	nono decimo
	undevicesimus	undevicesimo
twentieth	vicesimus	vicesimo
twenty-first	vicesimus primus	vicesimo primo
twenty-second	vicesimus secundus	vicesimo secundo
...	...	...
twenty-ninth	undetricesimus	undetricesimo
thirtieth	tricesimus	tricesimo

Numbers in the twenties combine as do those from thirteen onwards but in the reverse order: "on the twenty-third" is "vicesimo tertio", and so on. "On the thirtieth" is "tricesimo" or "trigesimo", but the last day of any month is often referred to in the Roman style as "the day before the first day of the following month" (*vide infra*).

Strictly speaking, the correct word for "ninth" is *nonus* but post-Roman feeling was that the word ought to be more closely related to *novem*, the Latin word for "nine", and so the form *novo* was often adopted in place of *nono* for "on the ninth". Other variants will be found in the epitaphs: for example we find *septemdecimo* in **8** to mean "seventeenth", this being based on the word for "seventeen", *septemdecim*. Such variants are usually noted when they occur.

The Roman Calendar

The Roman method of expressing dates was peculiar to Rome but it is to be found in many of the epitaphs in this collection. Three days in each month had special names. These were the "Kalends" or *Kalendæ,* the 1st of the month: the "Nones" or *Nonæ,* the 5th of the month except for March, May, July and October when they fell on the 7th; and the "Ides" or *Idus* which were eight days after the Nones, that is, on the 13th, except in the four months named above, when they were on 15th. All other days of the month were calculated from one of these three, counting *backwards*.

The day immediately before each of the three was called *pridie*. So 12th June was *pridie Idus Iunias* (*prid. Id. Iun.*) while 30th September was *pridie Kalendas Octobres* (*prid Kal. Oct.*, "the day before 1st October"). [Notice that the name of the month is treated as an adjective, qualifying *Idus*, etc.]

The 11th June was however not the second day before the Ides, as we might suppose, but the *third*, because in calculating the number of days all three - 11th 12th and 13th - were counted in. Therefore to work out such a date as *vi Non. Mai.* we first note that the Nones of May fell on 7th, then we subtract not *six* but *five* from seven to arrive at the required date, 2nd May.

Occasionally we find such a date as *a.d. xii Kal. Aug.* in a memorial. Here *a.d.* stands for *ante diem*, "before the day", and the whole phrase reads "twelve days before the Kalends of August". July has 31 days so 1st August can be thought of alternatively as being the 32nd July: 32 - 11 = 21, and the date in question is 21st July.

Roman Numerals

The Roman system of writing numerals was an additive system, using letters of the alphabet. One was i, two was ii (i + i), five was v, six was vi, ten was x, eleven was xi, twenty was xx. In order to avoid lengthy numbers, subtraction was also used, so four could be written either as iiii (an earlier form, still seen on some clock faces) or as iv, "one less than five". Similarly nine is ix, twenty-nine is xxix. Most memorials have dates and ages written in capital letters, which are easier to read than lower case letters, especially since fifty is l, likely to be confused with i unless written as L. A hundred is C (*centum*), five hundred is D and a thousand is M (*mille*). So XLIV = 40 + 4 = 44, LXXVII is 50 + 20 + 7 = 77, LXXXIX is 50 + 30 + 9 = 89, and MDCCLXXIV is 1000 + 500 + 200 + 50 + 20 + 4 = 1774. The subtractive principle could see 49 written as IL, but it is far more likely to appear as XLIX = 40 + 9. Similarly 1799 is more likely to be written as MDCCXCIX than as MDCCIC.

The
52
Epitaphs

Requiem æternam dona eis, Domine,
et lux perpetua luceat eis

O Lord, grant them eternal rest,
and may light perpetual shine upon them

1. Westminster Abbey

SAMUEL JOHNSON, LL.D.
Obiit XIII. die Decembris,
Anno Domini
M.DCC.LXXXIV
Ætatis suæ LXXV

Samuel Johnson, LL.D., died on the 13th day of December in the year of our Lord 1784, aged 75.

Notes.

LL.D. An abbreviation of *Legum Doctor*, "Doctor of Laws". *Legum* is the genitive plural of *lex*, "a law", and *Doctor* is our own word "Doctor". The double L indicates a plural noun, just as we use, say, "pp." as an abbreviation for "pages".

Obiit Literally "he went to", with "death" understood. Another expression using *obiit* is *obiit diem supremum*, "he arrived at his last day". [*Vide* **24**.] *Obiit*, or *obijt* [*vide* **2**], however is normally used on its own to mean "he (or she) died".

Die This is the ablative singular of *dies*, "a day", the ablative here implying the preposition "on". Since xiii is "thirteen", we are being told that he died "on the thirteenth day". [Cf. the legal term *sine die*, "without a day (being fixed)".]

Decembris *December* is a Latin nominative: *Decembris* is the corresponding genitive, "of December".

Anno This is the ablative singular of *annus*, "a year", with "in" implied here by the ablative, so "in the year".

Domini The genitive singular of *Dominus*, "Lord", so *Domini* is "of (our) Lord", with "our" being understood.

Ætatis The genitive singular of *ætas*, "age". The genitive here follows the earlier *anno* and shares this word with *Domini*, so the full phrase is *anno...ætatis suæ*, "in the year of (his) age".

Suæ This supplies the missing "his". It is the feminine genitive singular of *suus* and agrees with *ætatis*, which is also feminine and genitive.

M.DCC.LXXXIV Is 1000 + 500 + 100 + 100 + 50 + 10 + 10 + 10 - 1 + 5 = 1784. Note that the smaller (in value) *i* in front of the larger (in value) *v* indicates a subtraction.

2. Offwell

HIC PROPE REQUIESCIT IOANNA,
UXOR THOMÆ SOUTHCOTT DE
KILMINGTON GEN: FILIA NATU
MAXIMA, GULIELMI ET ANNÆ
COLLYNS DE COLLWELL, ARMIG:
OBIJT 14 DIE DECEMBRIS ANNO
DOMINI 1696

Near this spot lies Joanna, wife of Thomas Southcott of Kilmington, Gentleman, eldest daughter of William and Anne Collyns of Collwell, Esquire. She died on 14th December A.D. 1696.

Notes

Hic prope Literally "here close by", but we often find "near this spot" in English inscriptions of the same period.

Requiescit This is the third person singular present indicative of *requiesco*, "I rest", so either "rests" or "lies" is a reasonable translation.

Thomæ Thomas is a Hebrew name, but Latin adopted it and treated it as if it were a first declension noun, with genitive *Thomæ*, "of Thomas".

Gen. An abbreviation of *Generosi*, the genitive singular of *Generosus*, "a gentleman", in apposition to *Thomæ*. "Gentleman" was a recognised social rank until the nineteenth century, granted usually to wealthy men who had acquired their wealth through commerce or the professions. Originally it ranked a little below *Armiger*, "Esquire", a title born by the lower ranks of the aristocracy, but the borders soon became blurred, especially as Gentlemen, like Esquires, were often entitled to bear coats of arms.

Filia...maxima "Eldest daughter". *Maximus* in fact means "greatest", the superlative of *magnus*, but its connection with age is indicated by the interposed *natu*.

Natu "by birth", the ablative singular of *natus*, a fourth declension noun, which in fact is found only in the ablative case.

Gulielmi This is the genitive of *Gulielmus*, "William". [Cf. "Guglielmo" in Italian.]

Annæ The genitive of *Anna*, "Anne".

Armig An abbreviation of *Armigeri,* the genitive singular of *Armiger*, "Esquire", in apposition to *Gulielmi*. *Armiger* was an armour-bearer in the Roman army; "esquire" came to English through French from the Latin *scutarius*, "a shield-bearer". Note that although *armiger*i here is placed after the names and residence of both William and Anne, it refers only to William.

Obijt This is the same word as *obiit*, and is pronounced in the same way, as "obi-it". It was common practice to write the second "i" of a pair as "j". The same treatment was given to the final "i" of Roman numerals, especially in legal documents and official sets of accounts, so that, for example, *viii* (8) was often written as *viij*. [Cf. also *filij* in **11**.]

14 If this were written in words it would appear as *quarto decimo*, the ablative of *quartus decimus*, "fourteenth", to agree with *die*, the ablative of *dies*, "day". We might therefore have found it written as *14°*. [Cf. *2°* in **3**.]

3. St. Thomas, Exeter

HIC JACET CORPUS ANNÆ VXORIS
THOMÆ NORTHMORE GEÑ QUÆ OBIJT
SEXTO DIE APRILIS AÑO DOM 1686
HIC JACET CORPUS ELIZABETHÆ FILIÆ
THOMÆ NORTHMORE GEÑ ET ANNÆ
VXORIS EJUS QUÆ OBIJT 2° DIE AUGU:
1683 ANNO ÆTATIS SUÆ SECUNDO

Here lies the body of Anne, wife of Thomas Northmore, Gentleman, who died on 6th April A.D. 1686.
Here lies the body of Elizabeth, daughter of Thomas Northmore, Gentleman, and Anne his wife, who died on 2nd August 1683 at the age of two.

Notes

Hic jacet "Here lies". *Jacet* or *iacet* is the third person singular present indicative of *iaceo*, "I lie", a third conjugation verb.

Uxoris This is the genitive singular of *uxor*, "wife", and stands in apposition to *Annæ*.

Geñ Another abbreviation of *Generosi*. The "tilde" over the "n" indicates that letters have been omitted. [*Vide* "Introduction".]

Quæ This is the feminine nominative singular of *qui*, "who". The first *quæ* refers back to *Annæ*, and so leaves us in no doubt as to which of Anne and Thomas died; the second refers to *Elizabethæ*.

Sexto die "(On) the sixth day". *Sexto* is the masculine ablative singular of *sextus*, "sixth", agreeing with *die*, the ablative singular of *dies*.

Año Dom This is a simple abbreviation of *Anno*, together with a recognised abbreviation of *Domini*.

Ejus *Ejus* or *eius* is the genitive singular of *is, ea* or *id* and means "his", linking *uxoris* with Thomas Northmore. Alternative words for "his" is *sui* or *suæ*, but these would refer back to the subject of the sentence, namely, Elizabeth. *Suæ* refers back to her correctly in the following line.

2° The superscript "o" indicates that this is an abbreviation of *secundo*, "second". In the same way, 6° could have been used for *sexto* above.

Augu This is an abbreviation of *Augusti*, "of August", the genitive of *Augustus*.

Anno...secundo "In the second year". The two words are linked grammatically as ablatives, despite being separated by *aetatis suæ*, "of her age".

4. Mamhead

M.S.
DOMINÆ
MARIÆ TERESIÆ LEACH
Vidua **SIMONIS LEACH** Equitis Balnei
Et
Filiæ Prænobilis Domini **THOMÆ**
CLIFFORD Baroni de Chudleigh
Quæ obiit 9 Octob 1715

Sacred to the memory of Lady Mary Teresia Leach, widow of [Sir] Simon Leach, Knight of the Bath, and daughter of the most noble Lord Thomas Clifford, Baron Chudleigh, who died on 9th October 1715.

Notes.

M.S. An abbreviation of *Memoriæ Sacrum*, "Sacred to the memory". *Memoriæ* is the dative singular of *memoria*, implying "to"; *sacrum* is the neuter of *sacer*, "sacred", and can refer to any non-specified thing. Here it refers to the memorial itself - *monumentum* - which is a neuter noun anyway.

Dominæ Mariæ Teresiæ are all genitive - "to the memory of..."

Vidua We should expect this to be *viduæ*, the genitive singular of *vidua*, in apposition to *Dominæ*, etc., just as *filiæ* is correctly genitive in the line below.

Simonis is the genitive of the Latin name *Simo,* "Simon".

Equitis Balnei Two more genitives: *equitis*, from *eques*, is in apposition to *Simonis*, while *Balnei* (from *balneum*) simply means "of the Bath".

Baroni The genitive singular of *Baronus*, in apposition to *Domini Thomæ*.

5. Manaton

A ☧ Ω

CINERIBVS ET MEMORIAE
GVLIELMI CARWITHEN A.B.
HVIVS ECCLESIAE
ANN XLIV RECTORIS
FILIIQVE NATV MAXIMI
IOANNIS CARWITHEN A.B.
EIVSDEM ECCLESIAE PASTORIS
VIXIT ANN LXXIV MENS I DIEB V
DECESSIT PRID KAL NOBR
ANN MDCCCXXIV

H.S.E.
MARIA CARWITHEN
CONIVX GVLIELMI KARISSIMA
DEFVNCTA XV KAL SEPT
ANN MDCCCXVIII
CVM AGERET AETATIS ANN LXXV

To the ashes and to the memory of William Carwithen, B.A., for 44 years Rector of this church, and eldest son of John Carwithen, B.A., Minister of this same church. He lived for 74 years 1 month and 5 days, and died on 31st October 1824.

Here lies buried Mary Carwithen, dearly beloved wife of William, who died on 18th August 1818 aged 75.

Notes.

XP These are the Greek letters *chi, rho*, the first two letters of χριστος, *christos*, "Christ".

A Ω These are *alpha* and *omega*, the first and last letters of the Greek alphabet. "I am Alpha and Omega, the beginning and the end." Rev. xxi, 6.

Cineribus et Memoriæ Here we have a variation on *Sacrum Memoriæ*. The *sacrum* is omitted, though still understood: *cineribus* is the dative plural of *cinus, cineris*, "ash".

A.B. *Artium Baccalaureus*, "Bachelor of Arts".

Huius "Of this", the genitive singular of *hic, hæc, hoc*.

Ann The first *ann* is an abbreviation of *annos*. Those preceding a number starting with M are short for *anno*, "in the year". [Cf. **35** and **43**, in each of which we find *per annos* for a period of time.]

Rectoris The genitive singular of *rector*, in apposition to *Gulielmi*.

Filiique The -*que* is "and" - "and (eldest) son".

Ioannis The genitive of *Ioannes* (often *Iohannes*), the Latin form of "John" (which explains the presence of "h" in "John").

Eiusdem The genitive singular of *idem, eadem* "the same".

Vixit ann "He lived for..." In this line we have *dieb* which must stand for *diebus*, the ablative plural of *dies*, "day", so *ann* must stand for the ablative plural of *annus*, which is *annis*, and *mens* must stand for the ablative plural of *mensis*, which is *mensibus*.

Decessit The third person singular perfect indicative of *decedo*, "I depart".

Prid Kal Nobr This stands for *pridie Kalendas Novembres*, "the day before the Kalends of November", i.e. 31st October.

H.S.E This may stand either for *Hic Sepulta Est* or for *Hic Sita Est*, both meaning literally "here buried is". If it were a man buried rather than a woman, then the "S" would stand for either *Sepultus* or *Situs*, the masculine form of the respective adjectives or participles. (*Sepultus* is the past participle of *sepelio*, "I bury", while *situs* is the past participle of *sino*, "I place".)

Karissima "Dearest", qualifies *coniux* "wife" and is the feminine nominative singular superlative of *carus*, "dear". It is rarely spelt with "K".

Defuncta XV Kal Sept *Defuncta* is "dead" and refers back to *coniux*, a feminine noun. *XV Kal Sept* is *XV Kalendas Septembres*, the fifteenth day before the Kalends of September. The counting includes 1st September as one of the fifteen days, so this takes us back to 18th August.

Cum ageret *Cum* here is "when" and is usually followed by a subjunctive verb when the action is in the past. *Ageret* is the third person singular imperfect subjunctive of *ago*, "I set in motion", but refers here to the passing of time. *Ann* is short for *annos*. The line can be translated as "when she had reached 75 years of her age", meaning either that she was 75 years old or that she was in her 75th year. There is some ambiguity here.

6. Staverton

S.M.

HENRICI FOX ATHERLEY M.A.

ANN XXIV PAROCHIÆ STAVERTONIENSIS

VICARII

QUI HANC ÆDEM

PROPRIO SUMPTU

MULTIS IN PARTIBUS

RESTITUIT

OBDORMIVIT AUG II MDCCCLXXIV

ÆTAT LXVIII

R.I.P.

FILIUS POSUIT

Sacred to the memory of Henry Fox Atherley M.A., for 24 years Vicar of the parish of Staverton, who restored this building in many of its parts at his own expense. He died on 2nd August 1874 aged 68. May he rest in peace. His son placed [this memorial].

S.M.

FRANCES ATHERLEY

Viri Reverendi

H.F.ATHERLEY

ut amantissimæ

Ita amatissimæ

uxoris

Quæ ob: Aug: X

MDCCCLVIII

R.I.P

Sacred to the memory of Frances Atherley wife of the Reverend H.F.Atherley. As [she was] most loving, so [was she] greatly loved. Who died on 10th August 1858. May she rest in peace.

Notes.

S.M. *Sacrum Memoriæ*, interchangeable with *M.S.* [*Vide* **4.**]

Henrici The genitive of *Henricus*, the Latin form of "Henry".

Stavertoniensis The suffix *-iensis* creates an adjectival form of "Staverton" or of any other place: *Atheniensis*, "Athenian"; *Londoniensis*, "of London". This is the genitive singular, qualifying *parochiæ*.

Qui "Who", referring back to *Henrici*, but nominative, not genitive.

Proprio sumptu "At (his) own expense", ablative of *proprius sumptus, sumptus* being a fourth declension masculine noun.

Multis in partibus It is common practice in Latin to sandwich a preposition between a noun and its qualifying adjective, the alternative word order *in multis partibus* being thought perhaps less elegant or possibly open to ambiguity. Here *in* governs the ablative plural of *pars*, "part"; *multis* is the ablative plural of *multus, multa, multum*, "many", qualifying *partibus*.

Restituit The third person singular perfect indicative of *restituo*, "I restore".

Obdormivit The third person singular perfect indicative of *obdormio*, "I fall asleep".

Ætat An abbreviation of *ætatis*, but notice that *anno* is quite omitted, so that *ætatis* is understood to mean simply "aged".

R.I.P. *Requiescat in pace*, "may he rest in peace". *Requiescat* is the third person singular present subjunctive of *requiesco*, "I rest", used in an optative sense, "may he rest". *Pace* is the ablative singular of *pax*, "peace".

Posuit "Placed", the third person singular perfect indicative of *pono*, "I place". What the son placed is understood to be the monument or memorial.

Viri Reverendi "Of the reverend man", the genitive singular of *vir reverendus*. The word "wife" - *uxoris* - is found four lines further down, and is genitive in apposition to *Frances*, which however is not given here any distinctive genitive form.

Ut...ita "As...so" Both *ut* and *ita* have a variety of meanings when used on their own, but when used in combination suggest a comparison or a balancing. Used with superlatives as it is here, the combination could read "the more...the more" so we might possibly translate the two lines as "the more she was loving, the more she was loved". There is some flexibility in interpretation.

Ob Short for *obiit*.

7. Teigngrace

Hic Jacit
JOSEPHUS CHALLIS
hujus Parochiæ Rector
qui cum Septuagessimum
sextum Ætatis Annum
compleverat Vitam hanc
mortalem in Terris.
pro beata et eterna
in Cælis felicissimo
morte commutavit
Decimo Die Septembris
Annoque Domini
1683

Here lies Joseph Challis, Rector of this Parish, who, when he had completed the seventy-sixth year of his age, exchanged, by most welcome death, this mortal life on earth for a blessed and everlasting [life] in heaven, on the tenth day of September A.D. 1683.

Notes.

Jacit An alternative (rare) spelling of *iacet*.

Cum...compleverat We saw earlier in **5** that *cum*, "when", usually takes the subjunctive when the action involved is in the past. Some classical authors chose not to follow this rule: here *compleverat* is the third person singular pluperfect indicative of *compleo*, "I complete".

Septuages(s)imum sextum Literally "the seventieth sixth".

In Terris...in Cælis Both these are plural ablatives of *terra* and *cælum* respectively, indicating that more is meant than just "land" and "sky".

Felicissimo The masculine ablative singular superlative of *felix*, meaning literally "most happy" in the sense of "fortunate" or "lucky", a challenge to the idea that death is a tragedy, and suggesting that, to the Christian, entry to eternal life must always be welcome. Note however that *mors*, "death", is feminine, and so "by most welcome death" should be *felicissima morte*.

Annoque "And in the year", the *-que* being a superfluous but allowable embellishment to any inscription. [Cf. **18**.]

8. Ottery St. Mary

Hic sepultus est Henricus Marker, Gen., ob. tertio Junii anno dni Mdccv ætatis suæ lxxxiii.
Et etiam Henricus eius filius unus e quatuor huiusce Ecclesiæ Gubernatoribus obiit die septemdecimo Septembris anno dni Mdccviii ætatis suæ lxiii.
Et etiam Elizabetha uxor Johannis Marker Gen. ob. vigesimo primo Augusti A.D. Mdccxi ætatis suæ

Here lies Henry Marker, Gentleman, [who] died on 3rd June A.D. 1705 aged 83. And also Henry his son, one of the four governors of this church, [who] died on 17th September A.D. 1708 aged 63. And also Elizabeth, wife of John Marker, Gentleman, [who] died on 21st August A.D. 1711, aged ... [!]

Notes.

Gen. Short for *Generosus*, *vide* **2.**

Unus e quatuor...gubernatoribus Literally, "one out of four governors", with *e* governing the ablative plural of *gubernator*. *Quatuor* is indeclinable and has no separate ablative form.

Huiusce An emphatic form of *huius*, the genitive of *hice, hæce, hoce*, but still translating as "of this (same)".

Septemdecimo A single word, derived from *septemdecim*, "seventeen". However in **38** we have *decimo septimo* for "seventeenth", which is more "correct" Latin, that is, favoured by the "best" authors.

Vigesimo primo This is the ablative of *vigesimus primus*, "twenty-first", the Latin for "twenty-one" being *viginti unus* or *unus et viginti*, "one and twenty". "Twentieth" is sometimes *vigesimus* as here, but more commonly *vicensimus* and most commonly *vicesimus*. All three forms are to be found in classical Latin. [*Vide* **13** and **52.**]

Ætatis suæ ... It was not uncommon for ladies' ages to be left out in memorials. Coyness about age frequently extended beyond the grave.

9. St. Martin's, Exeter

MEMORIÆ SACRUM

WINIFREDÆ BVTLER FILIÆ RICHARDI

PRIDEAVX DE THVBORONGH

IN COMITATU DEVON MILITIS

QVÆ FVIT CHARA CONIVX EDVARDI

BVTLER DE EXON MERCATORIS

QVÆ OBIIT. 27. IVLII. 1673

VIVIT POST FVNERA VIRTVS

Sacred to the memory of Winifred Butler, daughter of [Sir] Richard Prideaux, Knight, of Thuborough in the County of Devon, who was the dear wife of Edward Butler of Exeter, Merchant, [and] who died on 27th July 1673. "Virtue lives on after death". [_Vide_ **16**.]

Notes.

Winifredæ "Winifred" here has been given a Latin form by adding an "a"; _Winifredæ_ is the genitive of _Winifreda_.

Thuborongh A mis-copying of "Thuborough".

In comitatu Devon "In Devon county". _Comitatu_ is the ablative singular of _comitatus_, a fourth declension noun. _Devon_ is short for _Devoniensi_, the ablative singular of the adjective _Devoniensis_, agreeing with _comitatu_. [_Vide_ **6**, and cf. **40**.]

Militis The genitive singular of _miles_, "soldier, knight", in apposition to _Richardi_. This was the usual way of supplying the title "Sir".

Fuit "Was", the third person singular perfect indicative of _sum_, "I am".

Chara The classical Latin for "beloved" is _carus_; neither the Latin Bible nor the Roman Catholic liturgy uses _charus_. However the spelling with "ch" is common in memorial inscriptions, for no clear reason.

Vivit "Lives", the third person singular present indicative of _vivo_, "I live".

Funera "Funeral ceremonies, death". The accusative plural of _funus_, which is a neuter noun. Both the nominative plural and the accusative plural of neuter nouns end in -a.

Virtus This has a variety of meanings: "manly excellence", "courage", "virtue". In a woman it may be taken to mean moral excellence, "the womanly virtues".

[**Vivit post funera virtus** was originally an apophthegm of Tiberius Caesar, and was the motto of at least five families of noble descent in Britain. It is not uncommon to find it used as a kind of cheering afterthought in memorials, as an alternative to the darker *Memento Mori* (*vide* **38**).]

10. St. Saviour's, Dartmouth

**Subter hoc marmor requiescit quicquid mortale fuit
Rice Price Higgins Armigeri.
Vixit annos LXXXVIII. Recessit sine prole
Die octodec: Novem: anno Domini
MDCCCXLVII
Animæ Ejus misereatur Deus.**

**Hoc monumentum Rice Giles Higgins
(Fratris filius) amoris causâ ponendum curavit.**

**In eodem sepulchro dormit quoq: spe resurrectionis
Maria Hayman
Uxor supradicti Rice Price Higgins.
Obiit Die undec: Maiæ MDCCCXXX
Ætat: LXIX**

Below this marble rests whatever was mortal of Rice Price Higgins, Esquire.   He lived for 88 years and died without issue on 18th November A.D. 1847. May God have mercy on his soul.

Rice Giles Higgins (his brother's son) caused this monument to be placed as a token of affection.

Also in the same tomb sleeps in hope of resurrection Maria Hayman, wife of the above Rice Price Higgins, who died on 11th May 1830 aged 69.

<u>Notes</u>.

Subter hoc marmor *Marmor* is neuter, so takes *hoc* for "this". Its literal meaning is "marble", but it may be used to denote any memorial stone. However, the phrase should read *subter hoc marmore*, where *marmore* is the ablative singular of *marmor*, governed by *subter* used to denote position rather than movement. It is likely that the form shown here is influenced by the (correct) phrase *iuxta hoc marmor* [*vide* **26**].

Quicquid The neuter nominative of *quisquis*, "whatever".

Mortale The neuter nominative of *mortalis*, qualifying *quicquid*.

Armigeri None of Rice, Price or Higgins takes a case ending: *armigeri* reminds us that if they did they would all be genitive.

Recessit The third person singular perfect indicative of *recedo*, "I depart, vanish, disappear".

Sine prole "Without offspring", a legal term. *Prole* is the ablative singular of *proles*. Cf. *sine exitu*, "without issue", in **28**.

Octodec: Short for *octodecim*o, "on the eighteenth", but note that the "approved" term in Latin for eighteen was *duodeviginti*, "two from twenty", and for "eighteenth", *duodevicesimus*.

Animæ "The soul" can be either *animus* (masculine) or *anima* (feminine). There seems to be a tendency to prefer *anima*. Here *animæ* is genitive, since *misereor* usually governs the genitive.

Misereatur "May (he) have pity on", is the third person singular present subjunctive of *misereor*, a deponent verb.

Causâ "For the sake of, on account of". Both the nominative and the ablative of first declension nouns end in "a"; it is not uncommon for the ablative to be indicated by a circumflex accent over this "a". [Cf. the phrase *honoris causâ,* "as a token of respect".]

Ponendum The gerundive of *pono*, "I place". *Ponendum curavit* is an alternative to *poni curavit* [*vide* **23**], where *poni* is the passive infinitive of *pono*. Both mean "caused to be placed".

Eodem The masculine ablative singular of *idem*, "the same".

Quoq. Short for *quoque*, "also".

Spe resurrectionis "In hope of resurrection". *Spe* is the ablative singular of *spes*, "hope", with "in" implied.

Supradicti The masculine genitive singular of *supradictus*.

Undec. Short for *undecimo*, the masculine ablative of *undecimus*, "eleventh".

Maiæ The genitive of *Maia*, taken to be "the month of May", although "May", *Maius*, is masculine in Latin, so this should be *Maii*. [Cf. **18**].

11. Thorverton

IN MEMORIAM
ROGERI TUCKFIELD DE RADDON COURT
ARMIGERI ET MARIÆ UXORIS QUI DEO
VOCANTE   FELICITER   EX   HÂC   VITÂ
ILLA   22   JANUARIJ   1677   ÆTAT   72
ILLE   22   JANUARIJ   1683   ÆTAT   78
IN MELIOREM TRANSMIGRARUNT

HIC ETIAM DORMIT JOHAÑES ROGERI
FILIJ NATU MAXIMI ET DE RADDON
COURT ARMIGERI PRIMOGENITUS QUI
TRIMESTRIS PRÆPROPERÂ MORTE RAP-
TUS TUTISSIMAS IN TUMULO INVENIT
CUNAS 15 JULIJ 1681

In memory of Roger Tuckfield of Raddon Court, Esquire, and of Mary [his] wife, who, God calling [them], joyfully made the journey out of this life into a better [one], she on 22nd January 1677, aged 72, he on 22nd January 1683 aged 78.

Here also sleeps John, first-born child of the eldest son of Roger and [also] of Raddon Court, Esquire, who, snatched by impatient death at three months old, found in the tomb the safest of cradles, 15th July 1681.

Notes.

Qui...transmigrarunt *Qui* is nominative plural, embracing both Roger and Mary. *Transmigrarunt* is a contraction of the more usual *transmigraverunt*, the third person plural perfect indicative of *transmigro*, "I make a journey". [Notice the Latin preference for placing the verb right at the end of the sentence.]

Deo vocante "God calling". This is an "ablative absolute" construction, free (absolved) from the main sentence, comprising a noun and a participle both in the ablative case.

Ex hâc vitâ *Hâc* and *vitâ* are both ablative, following *ex*. This is shown by a circumflex accent over each "a". [*Vide* note on *causâ* in **10**.]

Illa...ille Feminine and masculine of *ille*, "she...he".

In meliorem "Into a better", following on from *ex hâc vitâ* with *vitam,* "life", understood.

Johañes The tilde over the "n" indicates that this is a shortening of *Johannes*. The English order of words here might be *Johannes primogenitus filii natu maximi Rogeri armigeri* - "John, firstborn of the eldest son of Roger". The name of John's father is apparently unimportant: it is not mentioned!

Qui trimestris...raptus All are linked by being nominative.

Tutissimas...cunas These are linked by both being accusative plural. *Cunas* is the accusative of *cunæ*, a plural noun for a singular thing, "a cradle".

Invenit The third person singular perfect indicative of *invenio*, "I find".

12. Morchard Bishop

IN MEMORIAM

CHARISSIMI FRATRIS GVALTHERI
TVCKFIELD IN ARTIBVS MAGISTRI
ET HVIVS ECCLESIÆ RECTORIS
QVI MORTI OCCVBVIT XXIX°
NOVEMB: ANNO SALVTIS
MDCXXXVIII^o
MARIA PRIDEAVX
DEFVNCTI GVALTHERI SOROR
MOERENS POSVIT

INCERTVM QVANDO CERTVM
ALIQVANDO MORI

In memory of a most dear brother, Walter Tuckfield, Master of Arts and Rector of this church, who succumbed to death on 29th November in the year of [our] Salvation 1638.

Mary Prideaux, sister of the deceased Walter, sorrowing, placed [this memorial].

"It is uncertain when, though certain at some time, we shall die."

Notes.

Charissimi The masculine genitive singular of *carissimus*, spelt with "ch" as was common in inscriptions of this period. *Vide* note on *chara*, **9**.

Gualtheri The genitive of *Gualtherus*, a Latinised form of "Walter".

In artibus magistri Elsewhere written as *A.M.,* which is sometimes expanded as *Artium Magister*, "Master of Arts". Here *magistri* is the genitive singular of *magister*, in apposition to *Gualtheri*, while *artibus* is the ablative plural of *ars*, giving "Master in Arts".

Morti The dative singular of *mors*, "to death".

Occubuit The third person singular perfect indicative of *occumbo*, "I fall down", an alternative to *succubuit*. [*Vide* **13**].

XXIX° The superscript "o" indicates that this stands for *undetricesimo*, "twenty-ninth". [*Vide* **39**.]

Anno Salutis An alternative to *Anno Domini, salutis* being the genitive singular of *salus*, "salvation". It frequently appears as *A.S.*

MDCXXXVIII^{o} The superscript "o" is a rare reminder that the year number has to agree with *anno*, and so has to be in the ablative case. Even if this were written simply as 1638 in the original, this number would stand not for *mille sexcenti triginta et octo* (1638) but for *millesimo sexcentesimo tricesimo octavo* (1638th), qualifying *anno*. This applies not only to dates but also to ages; *vide* **36**, note on *XXV*$_{b}$.

Soror moerens In apposition to *Maria*. Note that to conform to classical practice, *moerens* should be *mærens*.

[Incertum quando, certum aliquando, mori Literally "Uncertain at what time, certain at some time, to die". A neatly balanced aphorism.]

13. St. Saviour's, Dartmouth

Memoriæ Sacrum
Rogeri Vavasor Qui fortiter
Se defendendo, & publico Patriæ
Inimico oppugnando magnanimæ
Succubuit Morti
Vicesimo octavo Die Mensis Martij
Anno **Dom 1696**

Ætat 34

Et
Iuxta hunc Locum
Conduntur Reliquiæ
Henrici Vavasor Filii
Vnici Rogeri supradicti
Spe Resurrectionis Generalis
Qui
Obiit secundo Die Mensis Sept
Anno **Dom 1727**

Ætat 36

Sacred to the memory of Roger Vavasour who, bravely defending himself and attacking the common enemy of the Fatherland succumbed to a hero's death on 28th March 1696, aged 34.

And next to this place are interred in hope of general resurrection the remains of Henry Vavasour, only son of the above-named Roger, who died on 2nd September 1727, aged 36.

<u>Notes.</u>

Se defendendo Literally "in defending himself". Although *defendendo* is ablative, *se* is not ablative but accusative, and so this is not an ablative absolute construction.

Publico...inimico oppugnando Again not an ablative absolute.

Succubuit The third person singular perfect indicative of *succumbo*, "I succumb". Cf. *occubuit* in **12**.

Anno Dom...Ætat An example of economy of writing, where *Anno* serves both *Dom(ini)* and *Ætat(is)*.

Conduntur The third person plural present passive indicative of *condo*, "I preserve, bury".

14. St. Olave's, Exeter

On a granite flagstone in the floor of the church.

ANNA
IOHANNJ GANDY
PRESBYTERO NATA
SVB HOC VELO
JACET VIRGO
ANNORUM 12
OBDORMIVIT
JAN 24 1659

Anne, daughter to John Gandy, priest. Beneath this covering she lies, a maid twelve years old. She fell asleep January 24th 1659.

Notes.

Iohanni...presbytero Both of these are in apposition, and are dative: "to John...priest".

Nata Literally "born", here meaning "daughter".

Annorum 12 "Of twelve years"; *annorum* is the genitive plural of *annus*.

15. Exeter Cathedral

HIC JACET
THOMAS BRANTYNGHAM, EXOÑ EPISCOPUS
NECNON TOTIUS ANGLIÆ ÆRARII PRÆFECTUS
CLYSTÆ DECESSIT EXEUNTE ANNO MCCCXCIV

Here lies Thomas Brantyngham, Bishop of Exeter, also of all England Lord Treasurer, who died at Clyst, at the end of the year 1394.

Notes.

Exoñ Short for *Exoniæ*, genitive of *Exonia*, the name the Romans gave to Exeter during their occupation of Britain. But *vide* note in **43**.

Totius The genitive of *totus*, "all", qualifying *Angliæ*.

Clystæ This is the "locative" of *Clyst(a)*. The Bishop's palace was at "Bishop's Clyst", some five miles outside Exeter.

Exeunte anno Ablative absolute, "the year (1394) departing". *Exeunte* is the ablative singular of *exiens*, the present participle of *exeo*, "I go out".

16. St. Martin's, Exeter

> IUXTA   HEIC   SITÆ   SUNT
> RELIQUIÆ   THOM: SPICER   &
> ELIZ. VXORIS   IUD: WAKEMAN
> VTRIUSQ FILLÆ ELIZ: BVTLER
> NEPOTIS   EDVARDI   BVTLER
> ELIZ: FILIJ   VNA CUM
> WINIFREDA VXORE

Near this spot are placed the remains of Thomas Spicer and Elizabeth his wife [and] of each of [their] two daughters, Judith Wakeman and Elizabeth Butler: [and] of [their] grandson Edward Butler, son of Elizabeth, together with Winifred [his] wife. [*Vide* **9**.]

Notes.

Heic This is a early form of *hic*, "in this spot, here".

Utriusq filiæ *Utriusq* is short for *utriusque*, the genitive singular of *uterque, utraque, utrumque*, "each of two", referring to *filiæ*. *Filiæ* is the genitive singular of *filia*. The family connections have to be unravelled carefully: Judith Wakeman must have been one daughter and Elizabeth Butler the other.

Nepotis The genitive singular of *nepos*. This could be either "grandson" or "nephew", but Edward Butler was Elizabeth Butler's son and hence Thomas Spicer's grandson.

Eliz: filij *Elizabethæ filii*, "Elizabeth's son". *Filii* is genitive in apposition to *Eduardi*.

Una *Uná* has an accent on the "a", indicating a long vowel. [This is elsewhere shown by a circumflex accent, cf. note on *causâ* in **10**.] *Unâ* could be either the ablative of *una*, "one", (feminine), or the adverb *unâ*, "together". The combination *unâ cum* with an ablative (*Winifreda uxore*) is a regular construction in Latin.

17. Colyton

HIC JACET

ELIZABETHA

UXOR JOHIS POLE

BARONETTI & UNICA ROG. HOW

MERCATORI LONDONIENSIS FILIA

OBIIT 16 DIE APRILIS 1628

TRES FILIOS TOTIDEMQ FILIAS

VIVENT^{S} RELIQUIT DVOBUS

INSUPER & FILIO & FILI^{A}

DEFUN^{C}

TIS

Here lies Elizabeth, the wife of [Sir] John Pole, Baronet, and only daughter of Roger How, Merchant, of London. She died on 16th April 1628. She left three sons and as many daughters living, as well as two, a son and a daughter, dead.

Notes.

Johis Short for *Johannis*.

Mercatori In apposition to *Rog(eri),* and therefore genitive. However *mercator* is third declension and should have as genitive *mercatoris*. Here it is treated as if it were second declension like *magister* or *armiger*.

Londoniensis "Of London", but an adjective, so literally "of a London merchant". *Vide* note on *Stavertoniensis* in **6**.

Totidemq Short for *totidemque* = *totidem* + *que*, "and just as many".

Vivent^{S} Short for *viventes*, the masculine accusative plural of *vivens*, referring to *filios*. The inscription had to be squeezed into an oval frame, which explains this abbreviation and the raising of a letter at the end of each of the next two lines down.

Reliquit The third person singular perfect indicative of *relinquo*, "I leave".

Duobus...defunctis An ablative absolute, with *duobus* and all words following (apart from *insuper* and *&*) in the ablative case.

18. St. Mary Arches, Exeter

Piæ memoriæ
Christophori Lethbridge armigeri
Hujus civitatis nuper prætoris. Simvl ac Mariæ uxoris
ejus
Qui post varia pietatis et Charitatis officia summa
fidelitate
Peracta placide in Domino obdormiverunt Hæc 15° Maij
Anno Doñi 1659: Ille 28° Julij Annoq: Domini 1670

To the pious memory of Christopher Lethbridge, Esquire, formerly Mayor of this city, and also of Mary his wife, who, after having completed with the utmost fidelity various duties of piety and charity, quietly fell asleep in the Lord, she on 15th May A.D. 1659, he on 28ᵗʰ July A.D. 1670.

Notes.

Piæ memoriæ Dative, "to..."

Prætoris The genitive singular of *prætor*, "a civic leader, chief magistrate", which exactly describes the office of a seventeenth-century mayor.

Simul Literally "at the same time".

Eius "His", referring back to *Christophori*.

Qui Plural, the subject of *obdormiverunt*.

Varia...officia...peracta The accusative plural of *varium...officium... peractum*.

Charitatis The genitive singular of *caritas*. Note the "ch" in place of "c".

Obdormiverunt The third person plural perfect indicative of *obdormio*, "I fall asleep".

Hæc...Ille Literally "This one (feminine)...That one (masculine)". [But also "the latter...the former". Cf. **29**.]

Maii "Of May". Here the month is taken correctly as *Maius*. [Cf. **10** and **23**.]

Annoq: Short for *annoque* = *anno* + *que*: "and in the year". [Cf. **7**.]

19. Exeter Cathedral

H.S.E.

GVLIELMVS KELLITT HEWITT

DE CASHOO IN PAR STAE ELIZABETHAE

APVD JAMAICAM INSULAM

ARMIGER

NECNON PACIS REGALIS CVRATOR

APVD *DVRYARD* HVIC CIVITATI ADIACENTEM

CONIVGI LIBERIS SOCIIS SERVIS PROPINQVIS

FLEBILIS OCCIDIT

III ID IVN A.D. MDCCCXII AET LV

Here lies buried William Kellitt Hewitt of Cashoo in the parish of St. Elizabeth in the Island of Jamaica, Esquire, also Guardian of the King's Peace [*i.e.* "Justice of the Peace"] in Duryard next this city. He died mourned by his wife, his children, his colleagues, his servants and his neighbours, on 11th June A.D. 1812, aged 55.

Notes.

In par stae Short for *in parochia Sanctæ*, "in the parish of Saint..."

Huic The dative of *hic, hæc, hoc*, "to this".

Adiacentem The accusative singular of *adiacens*, the present participle of *adiaceo*, "I lie adjacent to", qualifying *Duryard*, which is accusative following *apud*, although this is not apparent since *Duryard* (unlike *Jamaica, Jamaicam*) has not been given a Latin form.

Conjugi...propinquis All the nouns on this line are dative.

Flebilis occidit "He died mourned..." The phrase appears in an ode of Horace. *Occidit* is the third person singular perfect indicative of *occido*, "I fall down, die". *Vide* **24**.

III Id Jun *Tertio Idus Iunias*, "on the third day before the June Ides". The inscription reads *HI ID IVN*, but this makes no sense, and must be an error of the part of the stonemason. The third day before the Ides of June, which fall on the 13th day of the month, is the 11th, counting the 13th as one day of the three.

20. Sidbury

EXUVIAS SVAS CADVCAS, JVXTA HVNC
PARIETEM & VXOREM SVAM VNICAM
ET CHARISSIMAM, RICHARDVS
BABINGTONVS CLERICVS, PENE
OCTOGENARIVS, HVJVS ECCLESIÆ
VIGINTI ANNOS, PLVS MINVS,
OLIM VICARIVS, SPE FIRMA
RESVRRECTIONIS FVTVRÆ & VITÆ
ÆTERNÆ AÑO DOM 1682 DEPOSVIT

Next to this wall and to his only and most beloved wife, Richard Babington, priest, at the age of almost eighty years, formerly vicar of this church for twenty years, more or less, has laid his transitory remains, in firm hope of resurrection to come and of life everlasting, A.D. 1682.

<u>Notes.</u>

Exuvias *Exuviæ* were usually the external trappings of a man, his clothes, armour, etc. Here the term is extended to include the body as the external trappings of the soul. *Exuvias* is accusative and is the object of *deposuit*, the last word of the inscription.

Caducas Qualifies *exuvias*, with the literal meaning "destined to fall", as leaves in autumn.

Unicam Either "only, unique", stressing that Richard Babington, like Goldsmith's Vicar of Wakefield, had been a monogamist in the strict sense of the word; or possibly "unique" in the sense of "unparalleled, without equal".

Pene For *pæne*.

Plus minus "More (or) less".

Olim Further back in time than *nuper* (*vide* **18**); "once" rather than "formerly".

Futuræ *Futurus* is the future participle of *sum* "I am", and means literally "about to be", so giving us our own word "future". *Futuræ* is the feminine genitive singular, qualifying *resurrectionis*.

Deposuit The third person singular perfect indicative of *depono*, "I place, lay down".

21. Totnes

JACOBUS ROVIUS
EX ANTIQUA ROVIORUM FAMILIA
STIRPE OLIM CELEBERRIMA
HIC IN AGRO ORTUS
OMNIUM TESTAMONIO ORNATUS
ET VITAM IN ETERNAM
D.N.I.C.
EXPECTANS MISERICORDIAM PLENUS
MAGNO QUO VIXIT ANIMO
ANIMAM EFFLAVIT PLACIDUS
QUINTO SEPTEMBRIS DIE

A $\begin{array}{c}\text{Æ LXXXI}\\\text{S MDCCXIV}\end{array}$

James Rowe, from the ancient Rowe family, a stock once of greatest renown, born here in the county, honoured by the testimony of all, and hoping for mercy in eternal life from our Lord Jesus Christ, filled with the great spirit in which he lived. At peace, he breathed forth his soul on 5th September 1714, aged 81.

Notes.

Jacobus The Latin form of James.

Roviorum Literally "of Rowes", the genitive plural of _Rovius_.

In agro "In the county". _Agro_ is the ablative singular of _ager_, "land".

Omnium "Of all (men)", the genitive plural of _omnis_.

Testamonio For _testimonio_.

D. N. I. C. Probably _Domino Nostro Iesu Christo_, "from our Lord Jesus Christ".

Expectans For _exspectans_, the present participle of _exspecto_, "I hope for".

Animo The ablative singular of _animus_, "the spirit".

Animam efflavit Cicero used this phrase. _Anima_ is "the life force, the breath", rather different from _animus_. _Animam_ is the accusative singular of _anima_ and is the object of _efflavit_, the third person singular perfect indicative of _efflo_, "I breathe forth".

Placidus Literally "peaceful", an adjective, qualifying _Jacobus_.

A Æ...S _Anno Ætatis...Salutis_. The ultimate in abbreviations, with _Anno_ serving both _Ætatis_ and _Salutis_!

22. Axmouth

JUXTA
hic jacet
corpus GULIELMI SERLE
nuperrime de Bradford
in comitatu Sumerset
ARMIGERI cujus Proavi
olim et Avi jamdudum
de Godford in Aliscombe
in comitatu Devon fu-
erunt Qui Obijt 7mo
die Aprilis 1726
Ætat Suæ 71

Close by this spot lies the body of William Serle, most recently of Bradford in the county of Somerset, Esquire, whose ancestors long ago and forefathers now for a long time were of Godford in Awliscombe in the county of Devon. Who died on 7th April 1726, aged 71.

Notes.

Nuperrime *Nuper* means "lately, formerly"; its superlative *nuperrime* brings us closer to the present rather than further away.

Cuius "Of whom", the genitive singular of *qui, quæ, quod*.

Proavi olim *Proavi* (literally "great-grandfathers") were the first of the family to move in to Godford, many years ago.

Avi iamdudum *Avi* (literally "grandfathers") were subsequent generations who have continued for a long time to live in Godford.

Fuerunt The third person plural perfect indicative of *sum*, "I am".

7mo For *septimo*, "on the seventh", the masculine ablative singular of *septimus*.

23. Dunsford

In hoc cæmeterio cum longa serie majorum
sepultus jacet Baldewinus de Fulford
Baldewini et Annæ Mariæ filius et hæres
Regni et Ecclesiæ Anglicanæ (sicut omnes ejus proavi)
Egregius defensator
Obiit Westoniæ S. M. die mensis Maii secundo
A.D. 1871
Uxor ejus Anna Isabella amantissima et amatissima
Vitream hanc fenestram in memoriam poni curavit.
O Baldewine, magnum es mihi desiderium!

In this burial ground, in company with a long line of ancestors, is interred Baldwin de Fulford, son and heir of Baldwin and Anna-Maria, a most firm defender, (as were all his forebears), of the realm and of the Anglican Church. He died at Weston-super-Mare on 2nd May A.D. 1871. His most loving and beloved wife Anne Isabel caused this [stained] glass window to be placed in [his] memory. "O, Baldwin, thou art to me so great and grievous a loss!"

Notes.

Cæmeterio Properly *coemeterio*, the ablative of *coemeterium*, a word borrowed by church Latin from the Greek for a "resting-place, a place in which to sleep".

Maiorum Literally "of those greater (in age)", i.e. his forefathers.

Defensator A rare variant on *defensor*.

S. M. Clearly here *super mare*, "on sea", which is a harmless English classical pleasantry.

Baldwine The vocative of *Baldwinus*, used when addressing a person by name.

Es "Thou art", the second person singular present indicative of *sum*, "I am".

Mihi "To me", the dative of *ego*, "I".

Desiderium *Desiderium* is intense grief at the loss of a loved one, a yearning, a longing, or the object of such a longing. It is a term loaded with inexpressible undertones of desperate sorrow.

24. Salcombe Regis

LECTOR,

SI QUID BONI HABEANT

FIDELITAS, VIRTUS, ET PIETAS,

SI MORUM SUAVITAS,

ET FORMÆ ELEGANTIA

ADMIRATIONE SINT DIGNA,

HUIC CONDITORIO

RELIQUIAS ALICIÆ ROGERSON

DE *SALCOMBE* TENENTI,

REVERENTIAM NECESSE EST PRÆSTES,

VIGINTI FERME ANNOS NATA,

APRILIS 24.° 1795

SUPREMUM DIEM OBIIT.

FLEBILIS OCCIDIT,

NULLI FLEBILIOR QUAM I.L.GIDOIN

Reader, if there be any good in faith, virtue, and piety; if sweetness of nature and elegance of form be worthy of admiration; [then] it is necessary that you show reverence for this place of burial, holding the remains of Alice Rogerson of Salcombe. Very nearly twenty years old, she died on 24th April 1795. She died [greatly] mourned, but by none more than I.L.Gidoin.

Notes.

Quid boni Literally, "anything of good".

Habeant The third person plural present subjunctive of *habeo*, "I have". So *si quid boni habeant* is "If (faith, etc) should have anything of good..."

Sint The third person plural present subjunctive of *sum*, "I am".

Tenenti The dative of *tenens*, "holding", qualifying *conditorio*.

Præstes The second person singular present subjunctive of *præsto*, "I show".

Ferme The superlative of *fere* (*vide* **37**), nearer than "nearly".

Nata Literally "of the age of".

Supremum diem Literally "the last day". So in *supremum diem obiit* we have the full phrase usually shortened to *obiit*: "(she) reached the last day (of life)".

Flebilis occidit... In Horace, Odes Book 1, 24, we have *multis ille bonis flebilis occidit, nulli flebilior quam tibi, Vergili*, "by [lit. 'to'] many good men he died mourned, but none [was] more grief-stricken than you, Virgil". Here I.L Gidoin has adapted the quotation for his own purposes.

25. St. John, Exeter

M.S.
Catharinæ Filiæ Gulielmi
Chilcot clerici ob xiv
Cal. aug. mdcxcv
Nec non
ipsius Gulielmi Chilcot A.M. hujus
Ecclesiæ post nullum memorandi
Rectoris qui post annos vitæ
mortalis 48 revera cæpit
vivere 30° die Maii A.D. 1711
Αποθανων ετι λαλειται

Sacred to the memory of Catherine, daughter of William Chilcot, priest, died on 19th July 1695.
Also of the same William Chilcot, M.A., Rector of this church, second to none [worthy] to be remembered, who, after 48 years of this mortal life, truly began to live on 30th May A.D. 1711.
"Though he is dead, his voice lives on".

Notes.

Nec non   Usually written as one word, *necnon*.

Ipsius   "Of this same", the genitive singular of *ipse, ipsa, ipsum*.

Post nullum   The prime meaning of *post* is "after", which is the meaning it has in the next line down, but here it means "beneath", or "inferior to". *Nullus* is "nobody", so William Chilcot is "inferior to nobody", "second to none", insofar as his memorability is concerned.

Cæpit   For *coepit*, the third person singular perfect indicative of *coepio*, "I begin".

Apothanon eti laleitai   The Greek refers almost certainly to the fact that William Chilcot was the author of a small devotional treatise on "Evil Thoughts".

26. Shobrooke

IUXTA HOC MARMOR
POSITÆ SUNT RELIQUIÆ ELIZ UXORIS
HENRICI BACKALLER NATÆ 1638
DENATÆ OCTAVO DIE APRILIS 1698

HIC MORTALES IMMORTALIS SPIRITUS EXU-
VIAS DEPOSUIT SARAH FILIA PRÆDICTI
18 IANU: 1697/8

```
Flos ego vernus eram, sed flos erat iste Caducus
Sic cecidiq ut possem Surgere tectus humo.
Ne posthac recidam, me flos de Jesse Coronæ
Cælesti Inseruit nec datur unde Cadam
```

Near this marble are laid the remains of Elizabeth, wife of Henry Backaller, born 1638, died 8th April 1698

Here the immortal spirit of Sarah, daughter of the aforesaid, deposited her mortal remains on the 18th January 1697/8

"I was a flower of spring but that flower was born to fall.
So fell I, that sheltered by earth I might rise [again].
But so that I may not fall hereafter, Jesse's Flower has set me
In Heaven's garland, and it is granted I shall not fall from there."

Notes.

Natæ...denatæ "Born...de-born (died)." *Denatæ* is the feminine genitive singular past participle of *denascor*, "I perish", a deponent verb.

Mortales immortalis It is common to find two connected but contrasting words set side by side for dramatic effect. The word endings show that *mortales* qualifies *exuvias* and *immortalis* qualifies *spiritus*.

18 Janu 1697/8 Until the adoption of the Julian calendar in Britain in 1752, the legal year started on Lady Day, 25th March, whereas in the general mind the year started on 1st January. Any date between these two belonged therefore to two different years, in this case to the legal year which was still 1697 and to the common-sense year which was already 1698. It was not unusual to show both years in writing the date of events which occurred during the overlap. *Vide* also **49**.

Flos...caducus If we rewrite this line as *ego eram vernus flos, sed iste flos erat caducus*, then literally we have "I was a spring flower, but that particular flower was destined to fall".

Eram First person singular imperfect indicative of *sum*, "I am".

Erat Third person singular imperfect indicative of *sum*, "I am".

Sic cecidiq   *Cecidi* is the first person singular perfect indicative of *cado*, "I fall"; *q* is short for *que*, "and". The whole phrase is therefore "and in this way I fell".

Ut possem "That I might". *Possem* is the first person singular imperfect subjunctive of *possum*, "I can".

Tectus The past participle of *tego*, "I cover".

Ne...recidam "So that I may not fall (back)" or "lest I fall back". *Recidam* is the first person singular present subjunctive of *recido*, "I sink, fall again".

Flos de Jesse "The flower of Jesse", *sc.* Jesus.   Where the authorised version of the Bible, in Isaiah xi, 1, has a "branch" growing from the roots of the stem of Jesse, the Latin Bible has a "flower" growing.

Coronæ cælesti The dative *of corona cælestis*.

Inseruit The third person singular perfect indicative of *insero*, "I place in".

Datur "It is granted", literally, "it is given", the third person singular present passive indicative of *do*, "I give".

Nec "And not". It has been suggested that *unde*, "whence", is a miscopying of *inde*, "thence", and the above translation has been made on this assumption.

Cadam The first person singular present subjunctive of *cado*, "I fall".

27. Otterton

Sarah præcharissima
Roberti Duke Ar
filia et cohæres Rici
Reynell de Creedy Ar.
Obijt 2° Feb. Añ°. 1641
Reliquit fili $^{\text{os 3}}$
as 5

Sarah, most dearly beloved [wife] of Robert Duke, Esquire, daughter and co-heir of Richard Reynell of Creedy, Esquire, died on 2nd February A.D. 1641. She left 3 sons and 5 daughters.

Memoriæ sacrum
Rici Duke Ar: qui
Obijt 19. Apr. Añ°. Dñi
1641
Reliquit fili $^{\text{os 5}}$
as 2

Sacred to the memory of Richard Duke, Esquire, who died on 19th April A.D. 1641. He left 5 sons and 2 daughters.

Notes.

Præcharissima *Charissima* (properly *carissima*) is already superlative; the prefix *præ-* intensifies this: "most dearly beloved above all".

Cohæres At this period the question of succession and inheritance was of no little importance, and at a time when property normally passed through the male line only, it would be worth mentioning that a woman was co-heir to an estate, since this would enhance considerably her personal status. [*Vide* **29**.]

Rici Short for *Ricardi*, "of Richard".

Fili...os as An economy of lettering, whereby *fili* serves both *filios* "sons" and *filias* "daughters". The whole memorial is of interest for its intensive use of abbreviations.

28. Ottery St. Mary

> **Hic jacet Johannes Haydon de Cadhay, Armiger**
> **et Johanna uxor eius consanguinea et heres**
> **Johannæ Cadhay quæ fuit uxor Hugonis**
> **Grenvile Generosi qui quidem Johannes fuit**
> **primus Gubernator incorporatus huius Parochiæ**
> **ac obiit sine exitu novo die Martii Anno Domini**
> **1587 dicta autem Johanna obiit sine exitu**
> **decimonovo die Decembris Anno Domini 1592.**
> **pro quibus laus fit Deo**

Here lies John Haydon of Cadhay, Esquire, and Joan his wife, kinswoman and heir to Joan Cadhay who was the wife of Hugh Grenvile, Gentleman, which same John was the first Governor to be appointed to this parish and (who) died without issue on the ninth day of March A. D. 1587. The aforesaid Joan also died without issue on the nineteenth day of December A.D. 1592. For whom praise be to God.

Notes.

Heres Again we note the importance of a woman being heir to an estate.

Hugonis The Latin genitive of *Hugo*, "Hugh".

Quidem This would read better as *quidam*, "(a) certain".

Gubernator We have already seen in **8** that "governors" in Ottery St. Mary were governors of the church.

Sine exitu *Exitu* is the ablative singular of *exitus*, a fourth declension noun. Cf. *sine prole*, "without offspring", in **10**.

Novo The classical Latin word for "ninth" was *nonus, nona, nonum*. *Novus* is an often-found variation, clearly influenced by *novem*, "nine".

Autem "Also", can never begin a phrase or sentence, and is usually placed second, even if it then splits a seemingly integral phrase such as *dicta Johanna*.

Decimonovo This is not classical Latin. The two Latin words for "nineteen" were *novendecim* and *undeviginti* ("one from twenty"); "nineteenth" was *nonus decimus* or *undevicesimus*.

Quibus The ablative plural of *qui, quæ, quod*.

Fit The third person singular present indicative of *fio*, "I am made". The literal meaning of *Pro quibus laus fit Deo* is therefore "For whom praise is made to God".

29. Poltimore

M.S.

Ioannæ (Edwardi Ratcliffe
De B^d Clist filiæ,)
Uxoris Gul:^{mi} Bradford,
(Hujus Ecclesiæ Rectoris;)
Et Saræ, illorum filiæ:
Quæ,
(Brevi et difficili
Hâc peractâ)
Vitam inchoaverunt
Beatam et Immortalem:
Illa, An: Dom: 1722: Æt: 26:
Hæc, An: Dom: 1731: Æt: 9:
A Marito et Patre
P:
Suis ipse accessit IX Kal: Mart:
Ætatis LXIII
Anno
Salutis MDCCLIII

Sacred to the memory of Joanna, (daughter of Edward Ratcliffe of Broadclyst), wife of William Bradford, (Rector of this church); and of Sarah, their daughter, who (this short and perilous [life] completed), began their blessed and eternal life, the former in A.D. 1722, aged 26, the latter in A.D. 1731, aged 9.   [This monument is] placed by a husband and father.

He himself joined his own [family] on 21st February, A.D. 1753, aged 63.

Notes.

Illorum "Of them", the genitive plural of *ille, illa, illud.*

Quæ The feminine nominative plural of *qui, quæ, quod.*

Brevi et difficili hâc peractâ It would perhaps help the reader if this phrase were *Brevi et difficili hâc vitâ peractâ.* As the phrase stands, *hâc* must instead be read as "this one", depending for its interpretation, a shade tenuously perhaps, on the following *vitam,* which serves both for "mortal life" and, in *vitam ... beatam et immortalem,* for "immortal life". All words in the phrase, except for *et,* are ablative, and the whole phrase is an ablative absolute.

Inchoaverunt   The third person plural perfect indicative of *inchoo*, "I begin".

Illa   That one, further away, "the former".

Hæc   This one, nearer, "the latter". [Cf. **18**]

P.   This may stand for *positum*, "placed", the past participle of *pono*, "I place".

Suis   "To his own (family)", the dative plural of *suus*.

Accessit   The third person singular perfect indicative of *accedo*, "I approach". This verb is usually followed by *ad*, "to", an idea supplied by the dative *suis*. This seems an unusual way of saying "he joined" but this must be its import.

30. Exeter Cathedral

EDVARDVS COTTON S. T. P.

THESAVRARIVS & VNVS E CANONICIS

RESIDENTIARIJS FILIVS GVLIELMI COTTON

PRÆCENTORIS; FILIJ GVLIELMI EPISCOPI

HVJVS ECCLESIÆ; IN ARGVMENTO &

GENIO SVBTILIS; DOCTRINA PIETATE &

CHARITATE ANGELICVS AD DAMNVM

ECCLESIÆ & AD DOLOREM AMICORVM

VIZ: OMNIVM, OBIJT II° NOVEMBRIS ANNO

SALVTIS 1675

Edward Cotton, D.D., Treasurer and one of the Canons Residentiary, son of William Cotton, Precentor, [who was himself] son of William, Bishop of this church; shrewd in debate and in thinking, like an angel in doctrine, devotion and charity; to the loss of the church and to the sorrow of his friends, namely, of everyone, he died on 2nd November A.D. 1675.

Notes.

S. T. P.   *Sanctæ Theologiæ Professor*, "Professor of Holy Theology", replaced in time by "Doctor of Divinity, (D.D.)".

Filius   In apposition to *Eduardus*.

Filii   In apposition to the first *Gulielmi*, father of Edward, so fixing Edward as the grandson of Bishop William, a connection clearly worth mentioning.

Viz: For *videlicet*, "which means, namely", an abbreviation still widely in use in English.

II°   Assuming that II is the Roman numeral for 2, then this stands for *secundo*, "on the second"; otherwise *undecimo*, "on the eleventh".

31. Exeter Cathedral

HEIC SITUS EST

ROBERTUS HALL

IOSEPHI CL: EPI FILIUS PRIMOGENITUS

S S: THEOLOGIÆ DOCTOR FACUNDUS

HUJUS ECCLESIÆ. VIVUS THESAURARIUS

MORTUUS THESAURUS

VIVUS, MORTUUS,

RESIDENTIARIUS

OBIJT 29° DIE MAIJ 1667

ÆTATIS SUÆ 61

Here lies Robert Hall, eldest son of the distinguished Bishop Joseph [Hall], eloquent Doctor of Holy Theology. In his lifetime [he was] Treasurer of this church, [now he is] dead, [he is] a treasure. Living, dead, in residence [here]. He died on 29th May 1667, aged 61.

Notes.

Cl: This is almost certainly an abbreviation of *clarissimi*, "most distinguished", qualifying *epi(scopi)*.

Epi Short for *episcopi*, in apposition to *Iosephi*.

S S: This double S is an accepted abbreviation for *Sanctæ*, "saints", nominative plural of *sancta*; but *Sanctæ* here would in fact be genitive singular, qualifying *Theologiæ*. Nevertheless the composer of the inscription must have decided that SS would serve either purpose. [Cf. **30**.]

Huius ecclesiæ Despite the punctuation, this probably does not refer to Joseph, Bishop, or to Robert, though they were both of this church. The words seem more appropriately linked to *thesaurarius* and *thesaurus*. They are more importantly grammatically linked by the same order of words which gives us *huius ecclesiæ Rector* or its close equivalent throughout these epitaphs.

Vivus, mortuus Literally "living, dead". The whole of this part beginning at the first *vivus* is both an example of the conciseness of Latin and a witness to the gentle and affectionate wit possessed by the composer of the epitaph.

32. St.Margaret's, Topsham

Parcite Reliquiis (O Posteri)
Iosephi Et Elizabethae Maye
Qui Vitam sitientes aeternam
Mortalem Vobis non invide
Obierunt
1742

Do not injure the remains, O posterity, of Joseph and Elizabeth Maye who, thirsting after eternal life, [and] not envious of your mortality, passed on [in] 1742.

Notes.

Parcite Literally "spare", the second person plural imperative of *parco*, "I spare, refrain from (injuring)". Here the verb governs the dative of *reliquiæ*.

Posteri Literally "those who follow after", i.e. posterity.

Sitientes The nominative plural, agreeing with *qui*, of *sitiens*, the present participle of *sitio*, "I thirst after".

Æternam mortalem Both qualifying *vitam*; the accusative of *æterna mortalis*. Notice the juxtaposition of two related but contrasting words. [Cf. **26.**]

Vobis "To you", the dative of *vos*.

Invide It would be helpful if this were a misprint for *invidi*, the nominative masculine plural of *invidus*, "envious", agreeing with both *qui* and *sitientes*. The whole line would then read "not envious of mortal (life) to you".

33. Axminster

IN

MEMORIAM

DILECTISSIMI PATRIS,
BERNARDI PRINCE GEN^{SI}

NUPER DE ABBY, & MARIÆ CROCKER,
UXORIS EJUS 1^{MÆ} **DE LYNEHAM ORIUNDÆ:**
ET JANÆ DRAKE, UXORIS EJUS 2^{DÆ} **EX LONGO**

STEMMATE NATÆ; HOC MONUMENTUM, PIE-
TATIS ERGO JOHES PRINCE A.M. OLIM

VICARIUS DE TOTNES, NUNC DE
BERRY POMROY, D^{TI} **BERNARDI,**

ET MARIÆ FILIUS, MÆ-

RENS POSUIT

1709

In memory of a most beloved father, Bernard Prince, Gentleman, lately of Abbey; and of Mary Crocker, his first wife, sprung from Lyneham stock: and of Jane Drake, his second wife, of ancient and noble lineage; [to whom] John Prince, M.A., formerly Vicar of Totnes, now of Berry Pomeroy, and son of the aforesaid Bernard and Mary, through [filial] piety and in his sorrow, has placed this monument [in] 1709.

Notes.

1^{mae} Short for _primæ_, "first".

Oriundæ Literally "born of".

2^{dæ} Short for _secundæ_, "second".

Ex longo stemmate Literally "from a long family tree".

Natæ Either "daughter" or "born".

Pietatis ergo "on account of piety".

Johes Short for Johannes. The original has a tilde over the "h", indicating that letters have been omitted.

D^{ti} Short for _dicti_.

34. Tavistock

HONORATÆ SACRUM MEMORIÆ
IOHAÑIS GLANVIL HVIVS QVONDAM
IVSTICIARIORVM DE COMMVNI
BANCO: QVI MERITV FACTVS IVDEX
SVMO CVM LABORE ADMINISTRAVIT
IVSTITIAM, IVSTITIA CONSERVAVIT
PACEM, PACE EXPECTAVIT MORTEM,
ET MORTE INVENIT REQVIEM 27
DIE JVLII ANNO DOM 1600

Sacred to the honoured memory of John Glanvil of this [town] formerly of the Justices of the Common Bench, who, appointed a judge on his merits, administered justice with the utmost energy, by justice conserved the peace, in peace awaited death, and by death found rest on 27th July A.D. 1600.

Notes.

Memoriæ "To the memory", dative singular of *memoria*.

Meritu "Deservedly, by merit". This should be *merito*, an adverb derived from the ablative of *meritum*, a second declension noun.

Sumo cum labore *Sumo* is an abbreviation of *summo*. The phrase shows the regular order of adjective + preposition + noun.

Administravit...conservavit...expectavit...invenit All are the third person singular perfect indicative of their respective verbs; *administro, conservo, ex(s)pecto, invenio*.

Requiem The accusative singular of *requies*. This can mean either "rest" or "a resting place".

35. Widworthy

SPE beatæ resurrectionis
Subter conditæ sunt reliquiæ JACOBI SOMASTER
Viri probi et REI-MEDICÆ periti
Quam HONITONI novem per Annos feliciter exercuit
Ob Aug 28 1748 Æt Suæ 34°
JUXTA etiam requiescit ANNA prædicti Soror
Quæ ob. Mar 9° 1755 Æt Suæ 39°
SUÆ memor Mortalitatis
Hoc præeuntium Fratris et Sororis dilect^m M. P.
JOS^s SOMASTER hujus Eccles. Rec^r

In hope of blessed resurrection, beneath [this spot] are buried the remains of James Somaster, a man of upright life and skilled in matters medical, which he practised successfully in Honiton for nine years. He died on 28th August 1748 aged 34.

Beside [this spot] also lies Anne, sister of the aforesaid, who died on 9th March 1755 aged 39.

Mindful of his own mortality, Joseph Somaster, Rector of this church, has placed this monument [to the memory of his] departed [and] dearly-beloved brother and sister.

Notes.

Rei medicæ *Peritus*, "skilled in", may govern the genitive case, and this is the genitive of *res medica*, "a medical thing" or simply "medical science".

Quam The feminine accusative singular of *qui, quæ, quod,* referring to *res medica*, and also the object of *exercuit*.

Exercuit The third person singular perfect indicative of *exerceo*, "I practise".

34° Referring to *anno* understood, and representing *tricesimo quarto*, 34th.

Hoc...M. P. Presumably *hoc...monumentum posuit*. *Præeuntium* is the genitive plural of *præiens*, the present participle of *præeo*, "I go before", while *dilect^m* is an abbreviation of *dilectissimorum*, the genitive plural of *dilectissimus*. *Fratris* and *sororis* are both genitive singular, so the line would read literally "this monument of the going-before much beloved brother and sister...placed".

Jos^s Short for *Josephus*.

36. Sidmouth

I.H.S.
MEMORIÆ SACRUM
MARIÆ
UXORIS FRANCISCI ADDIS
LONDINII
QUAM TARDA SED CERTA ÆGRITUDO CONSUMPSIT
DIE XVI^{MA} **AUGUSTI ANNO DOMINI MLCCCXIV**
ÆTATIS VERO SUÆ XXV^{TO}
CHARISSIMA! QUAM COLUISTI LUGET
TE MARITUS TUUS
HEU PIETAS! HEU PRISCA FIDES!
UBI UNQUAM INVENIENT PAREM
REQUIESCAT IN PACE

Jesus the Saviour of Men

Sacred to the memory of Mary wife of Francis Addis of London, whom a slow but certain illness brought to her death on 14th August A.D. 1814 at the age of only 25.

Dearest! thy husband, whom thou caredst for,
mourns thee.
Alas for piety! Alas for steadfast faith!
Where will they ever find [her] equal?
May she rest in peace.

<u>Notes.</u>

I.H.S. *Iesus Hominum Salvator*, "Jesus, of men the saviour".

Quam The first *quam* is "whom", the object of *consumpsit*. The second *quam* should be *quem*, the accusative singular of *qui*, the object of *coluisti*.

Die XVI^{ma} This stands for *die sexta decima*, "the 16th day". *Dies*, "day", could be either masculine or feminine. In dates, as here, it was not infrequently treated as feminine.

Vero A versatile adverb, here suggesting "only".

XXV^{to} This stands for *(anno) vicesimo quinto*, "in the 25th (year)". The whole line is literally "in only the 25th (year) of her age".

Coluisti The second person singular perfect indicative of *colo*, "I take care of".

Prisca Literally "severe, stern"; but faith is "steadfast" in Paul's Epistles.

Unquam More commonly in classical Latin *umquam*, "ever".

Invenient The third person plural future indicative of *invenio*, "I find".

37. Kenton

IVXTA REPOSITVM IACET CORPVS DVLCEBELLÆ HODGES
CONIVGIS THOME HODGES DE SHIPTON MOIGNE IN AGRO GLOVC
ARMIG. VNIVS EX FILIABVS IOHANIS SYMES DE POVNSFORD
IN AGRO SOMERS, ARMIG. QVÆ DIVTVRNO MORBO LAN
GVENS CVM OPIS MEDICÆ BENEFICIO HYEME FERE TOTÃ
EXONIÆ TRANSEGISSET ILLIC VLTIMO OBIVIT FATO, VNICO
RELICTO FILIOLO AC NE DICAM QVANTO MARITI ET PA
RENTV DESIDERIO LVCTVO HOC ILLE LVBENS LVGENS INVITVS POSVIT
MORTEM OBIIT 17° DIE MARTII
A^{o} SAL 1628

Near [this spot] lies buried the body of Dulcebella Hodges, wife of
Thomas Hodges of Shipton Moyne in the county of Gloucestershire,
Esquire, [and] one of the daughters of John Symes of Pounsford in
the county of Somerset, Esquire; who, languishing through a lengthy
illness, and when she had sojourned for nearly a whole winter in
Exeter, with the benefit of all that medicine could offer, at last died
there, leaving behind a little son and I cannot tell what grievous sense
of loss to [her] husband and parents. He gladly, though sorrowing
against his will, placed this [monument to her memory].
She met with death on 17th March, A.D. 1628.

Notes.

Unius The genitive singular of *unus, una, unum*, and, as a pronoun, in
apposition to *Dulcebellæ*.

Opis medicæ The genitive singular of *ops medica*, "medical resources".

Hyeme...totã More commonly *hieme...totã*, "for a whole winter", the
ablative singular of *hiems...tota*.

Cum...transegisset *Transegisset* is the third person singular pluperfect
subjunctive of *transigo*, "I complete, spend time". The subjunctive is used
when *cum* is followed by a verb in the past tense. *Vide* **5**.

Ultimo obivit fato "Arrived at (her) final fate". *Obivit* is an alternative to
obiit. *Fato obire* was "to die a natural death", "submit to fate".

Unico relicto filiolo Ablative absolute, "a little only son being left behind".

Ne dicam "I may not tell". *Dicam* is the first person singular present subjunctive of *dico*, "I say".

Parentu This is short for *parentum*, the genitive plural of *parens*.

Luctuo This appears to be connected with *luctuosus*, "lamentable" and intended to qualify *desiderio*. It may well therefore be *luctuoso*, cut short.

Ille Referring back to *mariti*, i.e., the husband.

Lubens More commonly *libens*, "gladly". However *lubens* find its echo in the following *lugens*.

38. Madron

M.S.

GVLIELMI TREMENHEERE A.M.

QVI,

REVERENDI ADMODVM **GVALTERI BORLASE L.L.D.** NEPOS,

(HIC JVXTIM INHVMATI)

ET

HVJVS PAROCHIÆ VICARIVS NON VECORS

A DECIMO SEPTIMO CALENDAS DECEMBRES MDCCCXII

VSQVE AD VI ID JVL MDCCCXXXVIII

VITÆ DISCENDENTIS MORTIS ADVENTVRÆ ÆTERNITATIS EXPECTANDÆ

HAVD IMMEMOR

OCTOGENARIVS LAPIDEM SEPVLCHRALEM IPSE PONI CVRAVIT

A.S MDCCCXXXVII

"MEMENTO MORI."

Sacred to the memory of William Tremenheere, M.A., grandson of the most highly respected Walter Borlase LL.D. (buried close by here) and of this parish Vicar, not insane, from 15th November 1812 until 8th July 1838, who, by no means unmindful of declining life, of the approach of death and of longed-for immortality, an octogenarian, himself caused this sepulchral stone to be placed [in] A.D. 1837. "Remember you must die."

Notes.

Nepos This is a vague relationship, indicating grandson or nephew or just descendant. William Tremenheere was in fact both grandson and great-nephew of Walter Borlase, his mother and father being first cousins, the daughter and nephew respectively of Walter.

Vicarius non vecors This is a Latin pun. William Tremenheere had a reputation for eccentricity among his parishioners, and was clearly anxious to record permanently in stone the fact that he both knew of this and was determined to rebut it.

Decembres The accusative plural of *December*, used as an adjective, qualifying *Calendas*.

Discendentis For *descendentis*.

Immemor "Unmindful", is followed by (or in this case is preceded by) the genitive to supply the meaning "unmindful of".

Lapidem Normally "stone" but here used modestly for "marble", the stone in which the memorial is in fact carved.

Ipse "Himself". William Tremenheere was unmarried and had no immediate family, so he chose to compose his own memorial, leaving only the date of his death to be inserted when the time came.

Memento mori *Memento* is an impersonal imperative of *memini*, "I remember, bear in mind", a deponent verb. *Memini* can govern various cases, usually, like *immemor*, the genitive. Here it is followed by an infinitive *mori*, another deponent verb, "to die". The literal meaning of the instruction, "remember to die" is usually adjusted in translation to "Remember you must die".

[Walter Borlase was the eldest son of Lydia Borlase (*q.v.* in **50**) to survive infancy, and was vicar of Madron for half a century.]

39. Alphington

HUNC LAPIDEM PONENDUM CURAVIT

GULIELMUS BUTTERFIELD A.M. HUJUSCE PAROCHIÆ

RECTOR

IN MEMORIAM

REV^I GULIELMI BUTTERFIELD A.M.

FILII ADMODUM DESIDERATI

QUI UNDETRICESIMO ANNO PERACTO

QUARTO DIE ID JAN MDCCCLIX SUBITAM MORTEM OBIIT

NECNON

UXORIS DILECTISSIMÆ

ANNÆ BUTTERFIELD QUÆ SEPTUAGINTA ANNIS PERACTIS

QUARTO DIE ID OCT MDCCCLX

TRANQUILLE EX VITA DISCESSIT

NECNON IN MEMORIAM

EJUSDEM REV^I GULIELMI BUTTERFIELD M.A.

ANNOS VIGINTI OCTO HUJUSCE PAROCHIÆ RECTORIS

QUI OCTOGINTA UNO ANNIS PERACTIS

QUARTO DIE ID NOV MDCCCLXXIX

REQUIEM INVENIT

William Butterfield, M.A., Rector of this parish, caused this stone to be placed in memory of the Reverend William Butterfield, M.A., his greatly missed son, who died suddenly on 10th January 1859 at the age of twenty-nine.

Also of his most beloved wife Anne Butterfield, who peacefully departed this life on 12th October 1860 aged seventy.

Also in memory of the same Reverend William Butterfield, M.A., Rector of this parish for 28 years, who, on 10th November 1879, aged eighty-one, found rest.

Notes.

Huiusce An emphatic form of *huius*, "of this same (parish)".

Admodum This adverb imparts the utmost degree of intensity to any word it modifies. So "desperately missed" might well be a better translation than "greatly missed", but admissions of that intensity are not usual in English inscriptions. Latin allows feelings to be expressed with more abandon.

Undetricesimo anno peracto The ablative absolute of *undetricesimus annus peractus*, "the twenty-ninth year having been completed".

Subitam mortem obiit Literally "met sudden death".

Septuaginta annis peractis Another ablative absolute, "seventy years having been completed".

Discessit The third person singular perfect indicative of *discedo*, "I depart". Note how she "departed out of life".

Annos The accusative plural of *annus*, but translated as "<u>for</u> (28) years".

40. Bath Abbey

MEMORIÆ SACRUM
JOHAN: BOWLES ARM:
VICI DE DULWICH,
IN COMITATU SURRIENSI,
NUPER INCOLÆ;
CUJUS MORES INTEGERRIMOS,
INGENII VIM SINGULAREM,
JUDICIUM SANUM ET SINCERUM,
SCRIPTA SUA ABUNDE TESTANTUR;
QUEM EUNDEM CHRISTO FIDESSIMUM;
ECCLESIÆ ANGLICANÆ FILIUM OMNINO DEVOTUM,
LEGUM VINDICEM ACERRIMUM,
SIMUL ET ÆQUISSIMUM;
MARITUM DENIQUE OPTIMUM,
AMICUM NULLI SECUNDUM,
VENERATIONE VIVUM PROSECUTI SUNT
DESIDERIO MORTUI TENENTUR
CUM SUI, TEM OMNES BONI.
OBIIT ANNO SALUTIS MDCCCXIX,
ÆTATIS SUÆ LXVI

Sacred to the memory of John Bowles, Esquire, formerly a resident of Dulwich Village in the county of Surrey; to whose most upright character, to the singular force of whose talents, to whose level-headed and sound judgment, his writings are abundant testimony: who was held in the greatest respect in his lifetime as being most faithful to Christ, a wholly devoted son of the Anglican Church, a most energetic defender of the law, while at the same time just and impartial; in conclusion the best of husbands, a friend second to none.   Not only his family, but all good men accorded him the deepest respect while he was alive, and are seized by grief at his death. He died [in] A.D. 1819, aged 66.

Notes.

Abunde "In abundance, abundantly". The literal translation of *scripta sua abunde testantur* is "his writings abundantly testify (to)".

Testantur The third person plural present indicative of *testor*, "I testify", a deponent verb. Each of *mores, vim* and *iudicium* is an object of this verb, and hence is in the accusative.

Quem The accusative of *qui*, "who", and the object of *prosecuti sunt*. *Eundem* and all the nouns in this line and the following six lines which are accusative relate to *quem*.

Prosecuti sunt The third person plural perfect indicative of *prosequor*, "I honour", a deponent verb. The subject of this verb is jointly *sui* and *omnes boni*, but in translation it seems easier to use a passive construction here, especially as *sui* and *omnes boni* are also the subject of *tenentur*.

Legum Literally "of laws", the genitive plural of *lex*.

Nulli secundum "Second to none". *Nulli secundus* is the proud motto of the Coldstream Guards, and also of Lombard Banking, Ltd. [Cf. *post nullum* in **25.**]

Mortui The genitive singular of *mortuus*, "the dead (man)".
The Latin is literally "by grief of the dead man".

Tenentur The third person plural present passive indicative of *teneo*, "I hold, possess". This is a true passive and not part of a deponent verb.

Cum...tem A misprint for *cum...tum*, "not only...but also".

Sui "His (family)" - the nominative masculine plural of *suus*.

Omnes boni "All good (men)".

41. Littleham

M.S.
ROBERTI SUTTON ARMI
GERI QUI MORBO DIUTINO
AFFECTUS CRUCIATUS IND
IES INGRAVESCENTES IN
SIGNI PATIENTIA SUSTINU
IT VIRES SUFFICIENTE
CHRISTO OB PRID NON
MARTIS A.C. MDCCCV
ÆT SUÆ XXXIX MM POS
CONX LUCTUOSISSIMA

Sacred to the memory of Robert Sutton, Esquire, who, suffering from a long-lasting illness, endured the pains, worsening day by day, with remarkable fortitude, Christ supplying the strength . He died the day before the Nones of March [4th March] A.D. 1805, aged 39. His most sorrowing wife placed this memorial stone.

Notes.

This memorial is of interest for the way in which the stonemason has split some words and abbreviated others in order to fit the inscription into the space available. In fact in this epitaph it is perhaps helpful to be able to refer to an expanded transcription, with word breaks restored to their correct positions.

"M(emoriæ) s(acrum) Roberti Sutton Armigeri qui morbo diutino affectus cruciatus in dies ingravescentes insigni patientia sustinuit vires sufficiente Christo ob(iit) prid(ie) Nonas Martis A(nno) C(hristi) MDCCCV æt(atis) suæ XXXIX M(onumentu)m pos(uit) con(iu)x luctuosissima."

Morbo diutino "By a long-lasting illness".

Affectus "Afflicted", masculine nominative singular past participle of afficio, "I affect", agreeing with *qui*.

Cruciatus This is the accusative plural of *cruciatus*, "torture", the object of *sustinuit*.

In dies Literally "in days", but meaning "day by day"

Ingravescentes The accusative plural of *ingravescens*, "becoming worse", qualifying *cruciatus*.

Sustinuit The third person singular perfect indicative of *sustineo*, "I sustain, endure".

Vires The accusative plural of *vis*, "force", and the object of *sufficiente*.

Sufficiente Christo An ablative absolute, "Christ providing".

Prid Non Martis This should be short for *pridie Nonas Martias*.

A.C. As well as standing for *Anno Christi*, A.C. may also stand (after *Anno*) for *Æræ Christianæ* - "(in the year) of the Christian era".

Mm pos conx Short for *monumentum posuit coniux*, "(his) wife placed (this) monument".

42. St. John, Exeter

M.S. Chester Henrici Macmullen, scholæ Exoniensis alumni, Stephani Macmullen M.D. de Bridgewater in Comitatu Somerset filii natu maximi moribus egregiis ingenioque præstantissimo juvenis quem optimarum artium doctrinæque appetentissimum abstulit mors immatura die 18 Novembris 1824, ano æt 15. Quis desiderio sit pudor, aut modus tam chari capitis?

Sacred to the memory of Chester Henry MacMullen, a pupil of Exeter School, eldest son of Stephan Macmullen, M.D., of Bridgwater in the county of Somerset; a youth of noble conduct and of most outstanding talents, whom untimely death tore away from the most assiduous study of the best of art and learning on 18th November 1824, aged 15. "What shame or limit should there be in grieving for one so dear?"

Notes.

Henrici The genitive of *Henricus*, the Latin form of "Henry".

M.D. *Medicinæ Doctor*, "Doctor of Medicine".

Appetentissimum Literally "most desiring, most seeking after", describing the boy himself (*quem*).

Abstulit The third person singular perfect indicative of *aufero*, "I carry off".

Quis...capitis The frequently-quoted opening sentence of one of Horace's Odes (Book 1, xxiv). *Sit*, "it may be", is the third person singular present subjunctive of *sum*, "I am". *Tam chari capitis* is literally "of such a dear head", with *capitis*, the genitive singular of *caput*, "a head", standing (by synecdoche) simply for "person".

43. Clyst Honiton

Iuxta conduntur Reliquiae FRANCESCI WEBBER A.M.
Hujus Ecclesiae per XLIV annos Pastoris
S^{ct} Petri Cathedralis Exoñ Praebendarii
Et Parochiae de Stockley-Pomeroy Rectoris.
Qui per integerrimam Vitae Probitatem
Per ingenii Suavitatem eximiam
Pro Mores prorsus Christianos
Praecepta ista quae Concionibus tradidit
Exemplo Illustravit
Obiit Die 3^{tio} Novembris A.D. MDCCXXXVII Æ.S.LXIX
Memoriam omnibus Charisimam
Moerentibus Viduae & octo Liberis
Desiderium sui diutissime deflendum
Relinquens
Hoc Marmor Optimo Parenti Sacrum
Posuerunt Filii Pientissimi.

Next [this spot] are buried the remains of Francis Webber M.A., Minister of this church for 44 years, Prebendary of the Cathedral Church of St. Peter, Exeter, and Rector of the parish of Stockley Pomeroy. Who, through the most virtuous goodness of his life [and] through the remarkable sweetness of his nature, illustrated by his own example those precepts of his for unswerving Christian conduct which he urged in his preaching. He died on 3rd November 1737 aged 69, leaving a cherished memory to all, [and] to his sorrowing widow and his eight children the grievous loss of himself, forever to be mourned His most affectionate children erected this holy monument to the best of parents.

Notes.

S^{ct} Short for *Sancti.*

Exoñ Short for *Exoniæ*, "of Exeter".

Pro mores A probable misprint for *Per mores.*

Concionibus For *contionibus*, ablative plural of *contio*, "a sermon".

3^{tio} Short for *tertio.*

Charisimam For *carissimam.*

Sui The genitive singular of *se*, "himself" and referring to *desiderium*; "the loss of himself" or simply "his loss".

Filii Literally "sons"; the masculine ending masks the probable fact that daughters are included, so that the proper translation here is "children".

Pientissimi This is the superlative of *piens, pientis*, a rare variant form of *pius*, "dutiful, affectionate towards parents", found only in inscriptions even in classical times.

44. Rockbeare

M.S.

THOMÆ PORTER Armigeri

qui obiit die Octobris III A.D. MDCCCXV Ætatis LXVII

liberi hoc monumentum

D.D.D.

moerentes quod hoc Solum

frigidum quidem et angustum

pro tot beneficiis

pro vita data exculta amplificata

pro bonis moribus virtute religione

et voce et exemplo inculcatis

possint rependere

sperantes autem qua erga liberos

eadem eum fuisse erga Deum pietate

Deo, quod reliqui est, committunt.

Juxta sepulta est

SARAH ejusdem THOMÆ PORTER UXOR

obiit die Aprilis 1mo

A.D. MDCCCXXIII Ætatis LXIV

Sacred to the memory of Thomas Porter, Esquire, who died on the 3rd October, A.D. 1815, aged 67. His children have given and dedicated this monument, grieving that they can offer only this ground, cold and narrow as it is, [in return] for so many benefits, for life given, ennobled, made fuller, for good [qualities] of conduct, virtue and devotion inculcated both by precept and by example; and trusting moreover that the same devotion [he showed] towards [his] children [he had shown] towards God himself, they commit to God what is left. Next [this spot] is buried Sarah, wife of that same Thomas Porter, who died on 1st April 1823, aged 64.

Notes.

D.D.D. *Dono dedit dedicavit*, "gave and dedicated as a gift", but here plural: *Dono dederunt dedicaverunt*, with *liberi* the subject. *Dono* is the dative of *donum*, "a gift"; *dederunt* is the third person plural perfect indicative of *do*, "I give"; and *dedicaverunt* is the third person plural perfect indicative of *dedico*, "I dedicate, consecrate".

Quod The neuter of *quis*, "what", but meaning "that" after *moerentes*.

Exculta Literally "ennobled, refined", the feminine singular ablative past participle of *excolo*, "I cultivate", qualifying *vita*. Together with *amplificata*, this suggests a life not only given but developed both morally and mentally by careful parenting.

Bonis Literally "good things", qualified by *inculcatis*.

Et...et "Both...and".

Possint The third person plural present subjunctive of *posse*.

Sperantes...eum fuisse Literally "trusting...him to have been". *Fuisse* is the perfect infinitive of *sum*, "I am".

Eadem...pietate "With the same devotion", the ablative singular of *eadem pietas*.

Reliqui "The rest". We might expect some form of *relictus* here, but Cicero wrote *nihil est reliqui* for "nothing remains", and *reliqui omnes* is "all the rest".

45. Wimborne Minster

Hic subter in sepulchris conditi quiescunt
Thomas Fox, Iana Uxor, omnesque eorum Liberi,
Filius Nathanaelis Fox, de Poyntington
In Agro Somersettensi Rectoris.
Vir humili sorte conspicuus
Hujus Oppidi Pharmocapola haudquaquam ignarus
Scholæ Grammaticalis Gubernator minime indignus
Nec Sibi, nec alijs molestus.
In Conjugio fidelis, Paternitate benignus, amicitia
constans,
Socijs, Egenis, Omnibus
Comis, Munificus, Supplex.
Lege, Spectator, & Æmulare.
Obijt 25:to die Martii,
Ann: Dom: MDCCXXX
Ætat: 78

Buried in a vault below this place rest Thomas Fox with Jane, [his] wife and all their children. The son of Nathanael Fox, Rector of Poyntington in the county of Somerset; a remarkable man [though] of humble degree. A pharmacist of this town by no means unknowledgeable; a not unworthy Governor of the Grammar School; burdensome neither to himself nor to others. Faithful in wedlock, kindly in fatherhood, constant in friendship. To his colleagues, to the poor, to all, courteous, generous, and humble. Read, spectator and strive to be like him. He died on 25th March, A.D. 1730, aged 78.

Notes.

Eorum "Of them", the genitive plural of *is, ea, id*.

Sorte The ablative singular of *sors*, here "rank, station".

Minime The superlative of *parum*, "too little", and translated as "by no means". In answers to questions it may be used for "no". Its meaning overlaps that of *haudquaquam*.

Nec...nec "Neither...nor".

Paternitate The ablative singular of *paternitas*, "fatherly care".

Æmulare The second person singular imperative of *æmulor*, "I emulate", a deponent verb.

25:to Short for *vicesimo quinto*, "twenty-fifth".

46. Clyst St. George

Hoc Monumentum
Erexit GEORGIUS GIBBS
Hujus Parochiae, A.D.1708
ob Memoriam piam Majorum
Vid JOHANNIS GIBBS, Avi (Qui fuit
sopultus 15° July A.D. 1652, & At at
plus minus 82) Ansticiaeq uxoris nec
non GEORGIJ GIBBS, patris ejusdem G.
GIBBS (qui Contumulatus fuit 18° July
A.D.1683 Ejusq Aet quasi 81) et Aliciae
uxoris qui quondam in hoc templo
Solenniter Deum Venerari solebant

P.S.F.

George Gibbs of this parish erected this monument in A.D. 1708 to the pious memory of his forebears, namely his grandfather, John Gibbs, (who was buried on 15th July A.D. 1652, at the age of 82, more or less); and Ansticia his wife: also of George Gibbs, father of the aforesaid G. Gibbs, who was buried with them on 18th July 1683, (his age being almost 81); and of Alice his wife: who formerly were wont in this temple solemnly to worship God.

Notes.

Vid Short for *videlicet*.

Sopultus For *sepultus*.

July The stonemason has possibly mis-read *Julij*, and has substituted the English spelling.

At at For *Ætat(is)*.

Venerari The infinitive of *veneror*, "I ask reverently", a deponent verb.

P.S.F. A standard classical formula was *sua pecunia faciendum* - "he caused it to be made at his own expense", literally, "with his own money". *P.S.F.* may well therefore stand for *Pecunia sua fecit* - "with his own money he made (it)" or "this (monument) was made at his own expense".

47. Exeter Cathedral

M.S.

BASIL GUGLIELMI DOMINI DAER

DUNBAR COMITIS DE SELKIRK

FILII NATU MAXIMI

NOBILISSIMA STIRPE DOUGLASIA-HAMILTONIA ORTI

QUI PATRIAS VIRTUTES

SUAVISSIMA INDOLE HONESTISSIMIS MORIBUS

ORNAVIT

INGENIUM EXCELSUM

LITERIS BONIS ET SCIENTIA FRUGIFERA

FELICITER EXCOLUIT

GENTIS SUÆ SPES ET DECUS

HIC FLEBILIS OCCIDIT

CRUDELI TABE CONSUMPTUS

ANNO ÆTATIS XXXII A.D. MDCCXCIV

Sacred to the memory of Basil William, Lord Daer, eldest son of Dunbar, Earl of Selkirk, sprung from the most noble Douglas-Hamilton stock, who embellished his native courage with a most sweet nature and the most honourable conduct. He successfully cultivated his high talent through the study of literature and with fruitful learning. The hope and glory of his race, he died here deeply mourned, struck down by a cruel disease, aged 32, A.D. 1794.

Notes.

Literis bonis Literally "by good letters", which are literature.

Excoluit The third person singular perfect indicative of *excolo*, "I cultivate". [Cf. *exculta* in **44**.]

Gentis suæ The genitive singular of *gens sua*. *Gens* is more than mere family; here it could be "clan" and it particularly implies the existence of a blood-line, and of the pressing need to continue that blood-line

Decus This embraces all that is noble and praiseworthy in a thing or in a person, "grace, ornament, glory". It appears on the rim of the English pound coin, part of a quotation from Virgil's *Æneid*.

Consumptus The masculine nominative singular past participle of *consumo*, "I consume, destroy".

48. St. Petrock's, Exeter

P.M.
FRANCISCI ET ALEXANDRI
WORTH FILIORVM HEN: WORTH
DE WORTH IN AGRO DEVON ARMIGE
ILLE IN COMMVNE CONCILIVM CIVITATIS EXON
MERITISSIME ASCITVS DE CIVIBVS OPTIME
MERVIT QVIBVS INGENTEM SPEM SVI NOMINIS
EXCITAVERAT 9 DIE IVLIJ 1675 DESIDERATISSIMVS
OBIJT
HIC VERO NATV NON VIRTVTE MINOR IUVENIS
LECTISSIMVS SVMMO CVM SVORVM DOLORE
VITAM CVM MORTE COMMVTAVIT 18 DIE
OCTOBRIS 1680
H. M.
MARIA SOROR MOESTISS. EX TESTAMENTO
ALEXANDRI FRATRIS CHARISSIMI HÆRES
POSVIT
Hic etiam jacet Anna Worth eius^{dem}
Frañ que obijt 3^D Ap^s 1686

In pious memory of Francis and Alexander Worth, sons of Henry Worth Of Worth in the County of Devon, Esquire. The former, having been admitted most deservedly into the Common Council of the city of Exeter, gave excellent service to its citizens, in whom he had aroused great hope of his name. He died greatly mourned on 9th July 1675.

The latter, indeed younger by birth but not inferior in virtue, a most excellent youth, to the great sorrow of his family exchanged life for death on 18th October 1680.

Mary, their most sorrowing sister and heir by will to her dearly beloved brother Alexander, placed this monument.

Here also lies Anne Worth, [wife] of that same Francis, who died on 3rd April 1686.

Notes.

P.M. *Piæ memoriæ*, "to the pious memory (of)".

Filiorum The genitive plural of *filius*, simultaneously in apposition to *Francisci* and *Alexandri*.

Ille "That one, the former".

Commune The neuter accusative singular of *communis*, qualifying *concilium*.

Ascitus Also "foreign". Since the Worths lived near Tiverton, twenty miles from Exeter, they may have been seen as foreigners, but they were a prominent county family, and were clearly resident in Exeter, or their memorials would not have been placed in the city's churches. In any case "acceptance" makes clear sense in the grammatical structure here.

Meruit The third person singular perfect indicative of *mereo*, "I earn, win".

Excitaverat The third person singular pluperfect indicative of *excito*, "I arouse".

Hic "This one, the latter".

Minor This means "younger" as well as "less". "Perhaps less in years but not in virtue" is a possible translation, but it is clear that Latin has a semantic advantage here over English.

Suorum The genitive (plural) of *sui*, "of his (family)". [Cf. **40.**]

H.M. *Hoc monumentum.*

Moestiss. Short for *mæstissima.*

Ex testamento...hæres Heir by will rather than heir by primogeniture.

Que For *quæ*, "who", the feminine nominative singular of *qui*. By the Middle Ages the Latin used in legal documents in Britain had lost the *æ* ligature, this being replaced by *e*. The practice seems to have spilled over here.

3^{D} "Third". An English word has crept into a Latin inscription!

Ap^{s} *Aprilis*, "of April". The two bottom lines have been added later to the original inscription, and have been condensed and manipulated in order to fit into the space left at the foot of an oval frame.

49. St. Petrock's, Exeter

IN MEMORIAM CHARISSIMI PATRIS
GULIELMI HOOPER HUJUS CIVITATIS MER-
CATORIS HAUD VULGARIS NOTÆ CUM VIXIS-
SET AÑOS 65 URBEM HANC RELIQUIT IN
SPE MELIORIS NON MANUFACTÆ SED ÆTERNÆ
IN CÆLIS, OBIJT JANUARIJ 17° 1682/3
NON HABEMUS HIC MANENTEM CIVITATEM
SED FUTURAM INQUIRIMUS HEB: 13. V. 14:
BENJAMIN FILIUS A PRIMO SECUNDUS
AC PATRIS HÆRES MOERENS POSUIT

IN MEMORIAM
FÆMINÆ LECTISSIMÆ, CONJUGIS CASTÆ AC
FIDELIS, MATRIS PROVIDÆ, ET PRUDENTIS,
MARIÆ HOOPER FIDEI INTEMERATÆ, VITÆ
INCULPATÆ: QUÆ BONAM PARTEM ELEGIT
ET NUNQUAM AUFERETUR ABEA: NOVEM
LIBEROS PEPERIT ET DECIMUM PARTURIENS
ANIMAM DEO REDDIDIT 25° DIE SEPT 1658
MULIER TIMENS IEHOVAM IPSA LAUDABITUR
XXXI PROV: XXX

In memory of a most loving father William Hooper, merchant of this city, [a man] of no common mark. When he had lived for 65 years, he left this city in the hope of finding a better, not made by man but everlasting in Heaven. He died on 17th January 1682/3.
"For here have we no continuing city, but we seek one to come." Hebrews xiii. 14.
Benjamin, from the beginning the second son and heir of [his] father, in sorrow placed [this monument].

In memory of a most excellent woman, a chaste and faithful wife and a caring and wise mother, Mary Hooper, of unspotted faith and blameless life; who chose the better part, and never shall it be taken away from her.
She bore nine children and gave her soul to God in giving birth to the tenth, on 25th September 1658.
"...but a woman that feareth the Lord, she shall be praised."
Proverbs xxxi. 30.

Notes.

Vixisset The third person singular pluperfect subjunctive of *vivo*, "I live". [Cf. *cum ageret* in **5**.]

Memoris There is a feminine noun *memoria* for "memory", and an adjective *memor* for "mindful". Here we seem to have a feminine noun *memor* with genitive singular *memoris*, qualified by both *manufactæ* and *æternæ*. However, it has been suggested that the problem could be resolved simply by treating *memoris* as a misprinting of *memoriæ*.

Manufactæ Literally "made with hands", but should be two words, as in Acts xvii, 24: *Deus...non in manu factis templis inhabitat*, "God...dwelleth not in temples made with hands".

Januarii 17° 1682/3 For overlapping years *vide* note in **26**.

Filius...secundus...hæres There is a term *hæres secundus* meaning "second heir", but it might be argued that Benjamin was the second <u>son</u>, and heir to his father.

Providæ et prudentis *Providæ* is "having foresight", "prudent"! *Prudens* is "knowledgeable" or "wise".

Fidei intemeratæ A phrase used by Virgil.

Vitæ inculpatæ A phrase used by Ovid.

Bonam partem elegit... A reference to Luke x, 42: *Maria optimam partem elegit, quæ non auferetur ab ea*; "and Mary hath chosen that good part, which shall not be taken away from her". The author of this memorial shows a knowledge of the classical authors, but is unusual in making direct use also of the Vulgate Bible.

Elegit The third person singular perfect indicative of *eligo*, "I choose".

Nunquam The classical preference was for *numquam* rather than *nunquam*, but this changed subsequently. *Vide* also *unquam* in **36**.

Auferetur The third person singular future passive indicative of *aufero*, "I take away".

Abea Should be *ab ea*.

Peperit The third person singular perfect indicative of *pario*, "I bring forth, give birth".

50. Madron

Memoriæ sacrum
Lydiæ Borlase Christoph
Harris de Hayne Arm[i] Natæ
Johañ Borlase de Pendeen Arm[i]
Uxoris: Bis duos filios in Ecclesiâ
de S[t]. Iust Sepultos posuit; Quinque
filii et quatuor filiæ Supersunt. Piissimam
ejus et bene preparatam animam Mors
non abripuit Sed Cælo reddidit Iulij 28,
Anno Salutis 1725, Ætatis vero Suæ 54.
Amans, amabilis, amata, tam formosissima
quam dilectissima Sui generis. Viduum
reliquit charissimum viventis, hic labor-
antem et Suam dissolutionem expect-
antem, nullo modo post mortem
dividendum, Sed volente Deo, Sub
hac Sede adjungendum cineribus Suis. Animam fugientem
curet Iesus

Sacred to the memory of Lydia Borlase, daughter of Christopher Harris of Hayne, Esquire, wife of John Borlase of Pendeen, Esquire. She twice laid to rest two sons in St. Just Church; five sons and four daughters survive her. Death did not snatch away her most pious and well-prepared spirit, but returned it to Heaven on 28th July in the year of our Salvation 1725, aged only 54. Loving, lovable, loved; as beautiful as she was beloved, of her own family living she left a dearly-loved widower, labouring here and awaiting his own dissolution, in no way to be separated after death, but, God willing, his own ashes to be added [to hers] beneath this seat. May Jesus keep the departing soul.

Notes.

Natæ Literally "born", here meaning "daughter", in apposition to *Lydiæ*.

Bis duos Either "twice two" (equals four), or "on two occasions two..." Her two eldest sons died in infancy and were buried, one in 1690 and the other in 1691; two other infant sons were buried, one in 1697 and the other in 1710. Either translation of *bis duos* seems possibly to be intended.

Ejus "Of her", here used instead of *suam*, since *Mors* is the subject of the sentence.

Tam...quam "As...as"

Vero Again this versatile adverb, here suggesting "only".

[**Sui generis** A phrase adopted into English speech and writing, its equivalent in English being "one of a kind", that is, "in a class or genus of her own", "without parallel or equal"; but apparently not intended here, since otherwise *viventis* has no clear function.]

Sui generis...viventis Here *sui generis* means "of her own family" and *viventis*, genitive of *vivens*, qualifies *generis*: "of those of her family still living".

Dividendum "To be separated", the gerundive of *divido* "I separate", agreeing with *viduum*.

Volente Deo "God willing", an ablative absolute, familiar in English as *Deo volente*, abbreviated to D.V.

Adjungendum "To be united or joined to". Another gerundive, this time from *adjungo*, "I unite", and agreeing with *viduum*.

Sub hac sede "Beneath this seat". The memorial was placed above the family pew, beneath which presumably was the family vault.

Curet The third person singular present subjunctive of *curo* in an optative role: "may (Jesus) keep..."

Fugientem The accusative of *fugiens*, the present participle of *fugire*, "to flee, to depart". Virgil uses the phrase *anima fugiente*, "as his soul departed". One might be tempted to use the phrase "the fugitive soul".

[**Quinque filii...supersunt** Her eldest surviving son was Walter, vicar of Madron (*vide* **38**) who became Vice-Warden of the Stannaries, a post of great political power in Cornwall. Another son was William, who for fifty years was vicar of neighbouring Ludgvan, and author of works of the utmost importance and finest scholarship on the natural features of Cornwall, its archaeology and geology.]

51. Crediton

CONDITVR HAC VRNA FINCHVS QVI MAXIMVS ARTE
SVMMVS INGENIO MAXIMVS ELOQVIO
CONDIDVS ET DOCTVS TV THOMA FINCHE FVISTI
TEMPORA LÆTA DEVS TEMPORA DVRA DEDIT
EST TVA CONDITIO FÆLIX QVI FÆCIBVS ÆGRI
CORPORIS ABJECTIS GAVDIA MENTIS HABES
NON MIHI CORPVS ERAT VIVVM FVIT ANTE CADAVER
MORS VENIENS MORBI SVSTVLIT OMNE GENVS
TERRA TEGIT TERRAM MENS SVMMIS MENTIBVS HÆRET
OPTIMA MORS SALVE PESSIMA VITA VALE
QVI OBIJT 26 DIE JANVARIJ
AN DOM 1674 ÆTATIS SVÆ 51°

In this urn is buried Finch who [was] unsurpassed in character, supreme in ability, loftiest in eloquence.

Honest and learned thou wast, Thomas Finch. God gave happy times and hard times.

Thy state is happy [now] who, the dregs of an invalid body being cast off, dost possess the pleasures of the mind.

Not to me was the body living, before it became a corpse.

Approaching death took away every sort of disease.

Earth covers earth, the soul joins [now] with the highest souls.

Welcome, most kind death, farewell most miserable life.

Who died on the 26th day of January A.D. 1674, aged 51.

Notes.

Arte Literally "in art", but *ars* has many meanings and shades of meaning, as the dictionary will testify.

Condidus A word not found in the dictionaries. Probably a mis-spelling either of *candidus*, "shining white, sincere", or of *conditus*, "steadfast".

Thoma Finche The vocative of *Thomas Finchus*.

Fæcibus...abjectis An ablative absolute. *Fæcibus* is the ablative plural of *fæx*, familiar to us nowadays in its nominative plural, "fæces". *Abjectis* is the ablative plural of *abiectus*, the past participle of *abicio*, "I throw away, get rid of".

Gaudia mentis   Sallustius wrote of *gaudia corporis*, "the pleasures of the flesh".   *Gaudia mentis* are the antithetical pleasures, those of the mind or spirit.

Habes   The second person singular present indicative of *habeo*, "I have".

Vivum   Qualifies *corpus* (neuter nominative), "a living body".

Mors veniens   Literally "death coming", but perhaps better translated as "the coming of death (took away...).

Sustulit   The third person singular perfect indicative of *suffero*, "I suffer" and also of *tollo*, "I take away".   It is uncommon for two seemingly unrelated verbs to share the same form of the perfect tense, but it happens here.   The context favours *tollo* rather than *suffero*.   *Tollo* is found in the Mass: *Agnus Dei...qui tollis peccata mundi*, "O Lamb of God...that takest away the sins of the world".

[On the other hand, elsewhere in the Mass we are presented with *Agnus qui abstulit peccata mundi...;* "the Lamb who took away the sins of the world..." Here *tollo* has gone for its perfect tense not to *suffero*, which the dictionaries tell us it does, but to *aufero*!   Like any other language, living or dead, Latin is nothing if not flexible.]

Mens   Used here for "soul" in place of *animus*.

Hæret   The third person singular present indicative of *hæreo*, "I cling to, keep close to".

Optima...pessima   Literally "best...worst".

[**Thomas Finch**   Clearly in the eyes of at least one acquaintance, Finch was a most remarkable man, yet there appears to be no record elsewhere of who he was or what he did.   He was presumably a churchman of the very best kind, serving in a humble capacity either in Crediton or in the district around.   He remains an unknown but intriguing character.]

52. Gittisham

Adeste niuei Candidiq Lectores
Cum Lilijs ac Hyacinthis, libate lachrymas
tales eni deposcit Exequias Mellitissimus Ille Iuvenis
IOHANNES FIENNES, Hosp Grayensis Armiger,
IOHANNIS FIENNES de Amwell in Agro Hartford Arm
(secundæ sobolis a Patre suo Gul: Vicecomite Say & Seale)
Et Ipsius Vxoris Susannæ Filiæ
Et Hæredis Tho: Hobbes Hosp: Grayens: Armig
Fælix Filius Speratusq Pater
Qui perillustre FIENNORVM genus perennaret Posteris
Fuit nimirum
Adolescens ad Naturæ Normam perpolitus
Æque Corporis ac Animi Dotibus ornatissimus
Quibus vel a Pueritia
Prudentia senilis mores maritauit amænissimos
ut audiret sæculi par Decus, ac Deliciæ
Sed raro Præcoces diurnant fructus,
Du nimiu festinus ille surculus (futuru familiæ columen)
in Ætatis vernantis anno vicessimo tertio MDCLXXI
Cælebs, immaturâ morte præreptus est
Lugete Lachrymulisq cineres Ejus irrorate Præfieæ
Vos charites omnes et lugete Musæ.

Approach, ye readers, in garments white as snow,
with lilies and hyacinths, shed tears of grief,
for such are the obsequies for which that most delightful youth
JOHN FIENNES, of Gray's Inn, Esquire, cries out.
Of John Fiennes of Amwell in the county of Hertfordshire, Esquire,
(second child of his father William, Viscount Saye and Sele), and of
his wife Susannah, daughter
and heir of Thomas Hobbes, of Gray's Inn, Esquire,
A favoured son and one who, as a father, it was hoped,
would perpetuate the highly-distinguished line of the FIENNES
for posterity.
He was beyond doubt
an accomplished youth, a pattern of Nature,
furnished with the noblest gifts equally of body and of mind;

To which from boyhood itself
a mature wisdom married the most agreeable disposition,
so that he was reputed to be equally the glory and the darling of the
age.

But seldom do early fruits last for a day, and so,
as a too hastily-sprung shoot, he (the future head of the family),
in the twenty-third year of the spring of his youth in 1671,
unmarried, was plucked away by untimely death.

Lament, and with little tears moisten his ashes, ye Mourners,
all ye Graces, and weep, ye Muses.

Notes.

Adeste The second person plural imperative of *assum* (or *adsum*), "I am present".

Nivei candidiq(ue)   *Niveus* means "white as snow", *candidus* means "clothed in white".

Libate The second person plural imperative of *libo*, "I pour as a libation".

Exequias Should be *exsequias*, the accusative of *exsequiæ*, "a funeral procession", acting here apparently as an adjective qualifying *lachrymas* (which should be *lacrimas*).

Eni[m]... In order to fit this line into the space available, the stonemason has abbreviated *enim* (and *dum*, *nimium* and *futurum* further down) by omitting the final letter, each time indicating the omissions by a tilde over the previous "i" or "u".

Deposcit The third person singular present indicative of *deposco*, "I ask, beseech".

Hosp Short for *hospitii*, "of an inn", so "of Gray's Inn".

Fælix Should be *felix*, one of whose meanings is "making joyful".

Perennaret The third person singular imperfect subjunctive of *perenno*, "I last for many years". If *qui* is the subject, the verb is here used transitively, with *genus* as its object.

Ad...normam Literally "(made) to the rule".

Prudentia senilis A phrase from Cicero.

Maritavit The third person singular perfect indicative of *marito*, "I marry".

Audiret The third person singular imperfect subjunctive of *audio*, "I hear", used with *ut* to form a clause of purpose.

Ætatis vernantis Literally "of spring-like age", akin to the "salad years".

Vicessimo A variant on (correct) *vicesimo*. [*Vide* **8**.]

Præreptus est The third person masculine singular perfect passive of *præripio*, "I pluck, snatch".

Lugete The second person plural imperative of *lugeo*, "I mourn, lament".

Irrorate The second person plural imperative of *irroro*, "I moisten, sprinkle upon".

Præficæ Misspelt *Præfieæ* in the original, these were women hired to lament at the head of a funeral procession.

Charites One of the few words in the present collection of epitaphs legitimately starting with "ch", a transcription of the Greek χαριτες, "the Graces".

[**John Fiennes** was the eldest of the four sons of his father, Hon. Colonel John Fiennes, who himself was the third son, but at this time, the second surviving son, of the 1st Viscount Saye and Sele. Thomas Hobbes had lived at Amwell Magna, and presumably the house had come into the Fiennes family with Susannah, unless they were just close neighbours. The youngest son, Lawrence, became 5th Viscount in 1710, but he died unmarried and in the end the Viscountcy became extinct, although the Barony survived.]

The Word List.

The following word list contains all the words found in the epitaphs in this book (errors and omissions excepted, and with other exceptions noted below), together with others which are likely to be found frequently in other epitaphs. The following points should be noted.

Nouns. The nominative case of each noun is given, together with its genitive. The genitive is given either as a whole word, e.g. *ars, artis;* or as an ending only, e.g. *alumnus, -i;* or sometimes in an intermediate form, e.g., *ægritudo, -tudinis,* the full genitive being *ægritudinis*.

Verbs. Some (non-deponent) verbs are shown as their first person singular present indicative active, ending in *-o,* followed by the first person singular perfect indicative active, ending in *-i,* as in *cado, cecidi,* and *curo, curavi*.

Some first conjugation verbs are shown as above but with the ending only given for the first person singular perfect indicative, e.g. *commuto, -avi,* which in full would read *commuto, commutavi.*

Most verbs are shown in the form in which they appear in the epitaphs, followed by the first person singular present indicative in brackets, as in *abripuit (abripio)* and *abstulit (aufero).* This will allow the reader to find out more about the verb from a dictionary, where it is the usual practice to list verbs under their first person singular present indicative. The dictionary entry for *abripio* may read "*abripio, -rupui, -reptum 3*", indicating that the first person singular perfect indicative is *abrupui,* while the "supine" (which tells us how to construct among other things the past participle and the perfect passive) is *abreptum.* The "3" indicates that this is a third conjugation verb, so the infinitive must be *abripire.* The dictionary entry for *aufero* may read "*aufero, auferre, abstuli, ablatum 3*". This verb is also a third conjugation verb, but it is irregular. The infinitive cannot be inferred from any of the other forms, and so is listed specifically as *auferre.*

Adjectives. Very often the same word in English can be either a verb or an adjective. For example "accomplished" could be an adjective or it could be the past tense of a verb. There should be no difficulty in deciding the correct part of speech of any such word appearing in the word list. Verbs are distinguished in the list in the manner described in the previous section. Adjectives also have clear distinguishing features.

1. Adjectives which are like nouns of the first or second declensions are shown in their nominative singular masculine, feminine and neuter forms, e.g. *abreptus, -a, -um*, short for *abreptus, abrepta, abreptum*, and *aeger, -gra, -grum*, short for *aeger, aegra, aegrum*.

2. Adjectives which are like nouns of the third declension have identical masculine and feminine nominative singular forms, and so are shown in either of the two different forms following.

(a) If the genitive singular is the same as the nominative masculine/feminine singular, then the nominative masculine/ feminine singular is shown together with the neuter nominative singular, e.g. *brevis, -e,* short for *brevis* (masculine and feminine), *breve* (neuter). (The genitive singular is also *brevis*.)

(b) If the genitive singular is different from the nominative masculine/feminine singular, then these two forms are shown only, as in *amans, amantis* and *capax, capacis*. That is to say, *amantis* and *capacis* are the genitive singular forms for all genders, while the respective neuter nominative singulars will be understood to be *amante* and *capace*.

Missing Words. Some words occur in the epitaphs but nevertheless do not appear in the word list. For example the adjective *maximi* occurs frequently, but is not listed. If it were, it would appear just above *maximus*, of which it is a special case (most often masculine genitive singular). The reader is expected to make the obvious connection between *maximi* and *maximus*. On the other hand, *generis* is listed because it is alphabetically distant from *genus*, of which it is the genitive singular. It appears in the word list as *generis (genus)*, in this way indicating the connection for the reader.

Instructions The instruction *vide* ("see") is used to direct the reader to the expanded form of an abbreviation or to the more usual spelling of a word which appears in a variant form. Thus "dti *vide* dictus" indicates that "dti" is an abbreviation of a form of "dictus", in this case *dicti*; while "charus *vide* carus" indicates that *charus* appears in the epitaphs, but is to be found in the dictionary as *carus*.

"Jam *vide* iam" reflects the fact that mediæval (and more recent) authors favoured using "j" in place of "i" when it occurred next to another vowel or between vowels, whereas present-day (and Classical) practice favours the use of "i" at all times. Older dictionaries in fact had a section headed "J" under which appeared words such as *jam* and *juvenis*, but modern dictionaries list all such words under "I".

"Cujus *vide* cuius" directs the reader first to "cuius (qui)", and from there to the dictionary entry *qui*, of which *cuius* is the genitive singular.

Some adjectives are listed under their variant spellings, but to save space their different gender endings are not always shown. For example the list shows "moestissimus, etc. *vide* mæstissimus", saving space by omitting the *-a and -um* endings for each adjective.

Reference Numbers. The numbers in the word list are not page numbers: instead they show the number of the epitaph(s) in which a word may be seen used in context.

(a) If an epitaph number is in **bold type**, then the word will be discussed in the notes to that epitaph. For instance, *anima* is mentioned in the notes to epitaphs **10** and **21**, although it happens to appear also in several other epitaphs.

(b) If a number is in plain type, then the word usually appears in no more than three epitaphs, and may or may not be discussed in any of the notes. For example *antiquus* is found only in epitaph 21; while *autem* is discussed in a note to epitaph **28** and also appears in 44, but nowhere else.

(c) If a number appears in *italics*, then the word is to be found in more than three epitaphs, often in many more than three. The number shown is that of the *first* epitaph in which the word appears. Thus *de*, "of", appears frequently but does not warrant a note, and appears first in *2*. *Ætatis* on the other hand also appears frequently, but is mentioned in notes to epitaphs **1, 6** and **52**.

Words such as *amplius* and *animorum* which do not have a number against them are words which do not appear in any of the 52 epitaphs in this book. These 52 epitaphs were selected from a collection numbering more than a hundred; many words from the remainder of the collection have been included in the word list, and these the reader may well come across in other epitaphs. It is to be hoped that this book may therefore be something of a *vade mecum* to the itinerant seeker-out of new epitaphs.

Parts of speech. Usually there should be little or no doubt as to whether a word is a noun or verb or adjective, etc., especially after the reader has become familiar with how the word list works, and so there is generally no indication given of what part of speech a word is. Only if there is a serious likelihood of confusion is the part of speech mentioned, as with "siste (sisto) - stand still, pause (*imperative*)".

Latin-English Word List

a	from	29,50
ab	from	49
abea = ab ea *q.v.*	from her	**49**
abhinc	from hence	
abjectus, -a, -um (abicio)	despicable, thrown away	**51**
abreptus, -a, -um (abripio)	taken away, torn asunder	
abripuit (abripio)	snatched, dragged off	50
abstinentia, -ae	temperance, self-denial	
abstulit (aufero)	carried off	**42**
abunde	in abundance, abundantly, copiously	**40**
ac	and	*17*
accessit (accedo)	was added to, joined to	**29**
acerrimus, -a, -um	most keen, energetic, passionate	40
ad	to	30, **52**
adeo	to such a degree, so far	
adeste (adsum, assum)	come ye (to), approach	**52**
adiacantem (adiaceo)	adjoining, adjacent	**19**
adiungendus, -a, -um (adiungo)	to be united with, joined to	**50**
adjacentem *vide* adiacentem	adjoining, adjacent	**19**
adjungendum *vide* adiungendus	to be united with, joined to	**50**
administravit (administro)	managed, administered	**34**
admiratio, -tionis	wonder, admiration	24
admodum	completely	38, **39**
adolescens, -entis	youth, young man	52
adventurus, -a, -um (advenio)	to be about to arrive	38
adversus, -a, -um	adverse, poor, declining	
aedes, aedis	building	6
aeger, -gra, -grum	sick, ill	51
aegre	hardly, with difficulty	
aegri (aeger)	ill	51
aegritudo, -dinis	sickness	36
aegrotans, -tantis	falling sick, ill	
aemulare (aemulor)	emulate, strive to copy	**45**
aeque	in like manner, equally	52
aequissimus, -a, -um	most fair, impartial	40

aerarium, -ii	treasury	15
aetas, aetatis	age	
aetatis (aetas)	(of) age	**1, 6, 52**
aeternitas, aeternitatis	eternity, immortality	38
aeternus, -a, -um	everlasting, immortal	20, **32**, 49
affectus, -a, -um	weakened by	**41**
affectus, -us	condition	
ager, agri	county, district	
ageret (ago)	had reached, approached	**5**
agro (ager)	(in) the county of	**21**
aliquando	at some time	12
aliter	in any other way, otherwise	
alius, -a, -um	other	45
altiore	more highly	
alumnus, -i	pupil, undergraduate	42
amabilis, -e	lovable	50
amaenissimus		
vide amoenissimus	most delightful	52
amans, amantis (amo)	loving, affectionate	50
amantissimus, -a, -um	most loving	6, 23
amatissimus, -a, -um	greatly loved	6, 23
amatus, -a, -um (amo)	beloved	50
amicitia, -ae	friendship	45
amicus, -i	friend	30, 40
amoenissimus , -a, -um	most delightful	52
amor, amoris	love	10
amplificatus, -a, -um		
(amplifico)	enlarged, increased	44
amplius	more, further	
angelicus, -a, -um	like an angel	30
Angliæ	of England	15
Anglicanus, -a, -um	Anglican	23, 40
angustus, -a, -um	narrow	44
anima, -ae	soul, mind	**10, 21**
animorum (animus)	of souls	
animus, -i	soul, spirit	**21**, 52
annis (annus)	years	**5, 39**
anno (annus)	(in the) year	**1, 3, 39**
annoque (annus)	and in the year	**7**

annorum (annus)	of years	**14**
annos (annus)	years	**5, 39**
annus, -i	year	
ante	before	**51**
antehac	before this time, formerly	
antiquus, -a, -um	ancient, outstanding	21
appetentissimus, -a, -um	most desiring, seeking	42
apud	in, at (home)	19
argumentum, -i	debate, matter	30
arma, armorum	tools, arms (of war)	
arm(iger), armigeri	Esquire	**2, 10**
ars, artis	art, knowledge, character	42, **51**
artibus (ars)	in arts	**12**
artium (ars)	of arts	42
ascitus, -a, -um	foreign, from without	
ascitus, -us	acceptance	**48**
assiduus, -a, -um	continual, constant, steady	
at	but, moreover	
auctor, auctoris	creator, author	
audiret (audio)	might hear	**52**
auferetur (aufero)	will be taken away	**49**
aut	or, or else, rather	**42**
autem	also, however, moreover	**28**, 44
avus, -i	grandfather, ancestor	**22**, 46
balneum, -i	bath	**4**
bancum, -i	bench	34
baronettus, -i	baronet	17
baronus, -i	baron	**4**
beatus, -a, -um	blessed, happy	7, 29, 35
bene	well	50
beneficium, -ii	benefit, service	37, 44
benevolentia, -iae	benevolence	
benignus, -a, -um	kindly, benign	45
bis	twice, on two occasions	**50**
boni (bonus)	good men	**40**
bonus, -a, -um	good	**24, 47, 49**
brevis, -e	short	**29**

cadam (cado)	I (shall) fall	**26**
cadaver, cadaveris	corpse, carcase	51
cado, cecidi	fall	**26**
caducus, -a, -um	destined to die, transitory	**20**, **26**
caelebs, caelibis	bachelor	52
caelestis, -e	heavenly	**26**
caelis (caelum)	(in) heaven	7, 49
caelum, -i	heaven	7, 49, 50
caemeterio *vide* coemeterium	(in) a cemetery	**23**
caepio, caepi *vide* coepio	begin	
caepit *vide* coepio	began	**25**
cal *vide* Kalendae	the Kalends	25
calendae, -arum *vide* Kalendae	the Kalends	38
candidus, -a, -um	white, clothed in white, honest	**51**, **52**
candor, -is	purity	
canonicus, -i	canon	30
capax, capacis	ample	
capella, -ae	chapel	
capitis (caput)	of a head	**42**
captus, -a, -um	taken	
caput, capitis	head, person	**42**
carissimus, -a, -um	dearest	
caritas, caritatis	love, esteem	**18**, 30
caro, carnis	flesh	
carus, -a, -um	dear, loved	**42**
castus, -a, -um	chaste, pure, holy	49
cated(ra)	cathedral	
cathedralis, -is	cathedral	43
causâ	through, for the sake of	**10**
cecidi (cado)	I fell	**26**
celatus, -a, -um	secret	
celiberrimus, -a, -um	renowned, highly distingushed	21
certus, -a, -um	certain, sure	12, 36
cessit (cedo)	yielded	
chara *vide* carus	dear	**8**
chari *vide* carus	dear	**42**
charissimus, etc.		
vide carissimus	dearest	**12**, **43**
charitas *vide* caritas	love, charity	**18**, 30
Charites, -um	Graces	**52**

charus *vide* carus	dear	
christianus, -a, -um	christian	43
Christus, -i	Christ	40, **41**
cineres, cinerum	ashes	50, 52
cineribus (cineres)	(to the) ashes	**5**, 50
cinis, cineris	ashes	
civilis, -e	civil	
civis, -is	citizen	48
civitas, -tatis	city	*18*
clarissimus, -a, -um	distinguished	**31**
clarus, -a, -um	clear, bright	
clementia, -ae	mercy. humanity	
clericus, -i	cleric, priest	20, 25
coeli *vide* caelum	of heaven	
coemeterium, -ii	cemetery	**23**
coepio, coepi	begin	**25**
cohaeres, -haeredis	co-heir	**27**
collegium, -ii	college	
collocavit (colloco)	placed, disposed, arranged	
coluerunt (colo)	studied, frequented, worshipped	
coluisti (colo)	you took care of	**36**
coluit (colo)	cultivated	
columen, columinis	height, chief, pillar	52
com *vide* comitatu	in the county of	
comes, comitis	earl, count	47
comis, -e	courteous, kind, friendly	45
comitatu (comitatus)	(in) the county of	**9**
comitatus, -us	county	
comminutus, -a, -um	weakened	
committo, commisi	entrust, commit to	44
communis, -e	common, general	34, **48**
commuto, -avi	exchange	7, 48
compleverat (compleo)	(he) had completed	7
concilio, -avi	reconcile	
concilium, -ii	council	48
concionibus *vide* contio	by speeches, sermons	**43**
conditio, -onis	state, condition	51
conditorium, -ii	burying place	24
conditur (condo)	it is buried, etc	51

conditus, -a, -um (condo)	buried, etc.	35, 45
condo, condidi	bury, place, preserve	
conduntur (condo)	are buried, etc.	**13**, 43
confectus, -a, -um	killed, destroyed, weakened	
coniugium, -ii	marriage	45
coniunctus, -a, -um	joined together, close	
coniux, -iugis	wife, husband	5, **19**, 37
conjugium *vide* coniugium	marriage	45
conjunctus *vide* coniunctus	joined together, close	
conjux *vide* coniux	wife, husband	49
consanguinea, -ae	kinswoman, sister	28
conservo, -avi	conserve, keep, maintain	**34**
conspicuus, -a, -um	remarkable, striking, conspicuous	45
constans, -tantis	firm, steady, constant	45
constanter	firmly, courageously	
consuetudo, -tudinis	custom, habit	
consumpsit (consumo)	it consumed, destroyed, killed	36
consumptus, -a, -um	consumed, destroyed, killed	**47**
contio, -tionis	speech, sermon, address	**43**
contulit (confero)	joined	
contumulatus, -a, -um (contumulo)	buried with	46
conx *vide* coniux	wife	**41**
coram	in the presence of	
corona, -ae	crown, garland	**26**
corpus, corporis	body	*3*
creatus, -a, -um	created	
cruciatus, -a, -um	most painful, excruciating	
cruciatus, -us	torture, torment	**41**
crudelis, -e	cruel, merciless	47
cuius (qui)	of whom, whose	**22**, 40
cujus *vide* cuius	of whom, whose	**22**, 40
cultor, cultoris	worshipper	
cum	when	**5, 7, 37**
cum	with	**34**
cum...tum	not only... but also	**40**
cunae, cunarum	cradle	**11**
cunas (cunae)	cradle	**11**
cura, -ae	care	
curator, -toris	guardian, keeper	19

curet (curo)	may keep	**50**
curo, curavi	command, give instructions, keep	**10**
damnum, -i	loss	30
datur (do)	it is given, decreed, granted	**26**
datus, -a, -um (do)	given	44
de	of	*2*
debitum, -i	debt	
decem	ten	
decessit (decedo)	died, deceased	**5**, 14
decimonovo	on the nineteenth	**28**
decimus, -a, -um	tenth	*7*
decrevit (decresco)	waned, decreased	
decus, decoris	pride, glory	**47**, 52
dederunt (do)	gave	**44**
dedicaverunt	dedicated	**44**
dedicavit (dedico)	gave up, dedicated	**44**
dedit (do)	gave	**44**, 51
defendendo (defenso)	in defending	13
defensator *vide* defensor	defender	**23**
defensor, -oris	defender	
deflendus, -a, -um (defleo)	to be wept for	43
defletus, -a, -um (defleo)	wept for	
defunctus, -a, -um	defunct, deceased	**5, 17**
Dei (Deus)	of God	
dein(de)	after that	
deliciae, -arum	delight, darling, beloved	52
demum	at last, finally	
denatus, -a	dead (de-born)	**26**
denique	finally, in conclusion	40
Deo (Deus)	to God	**11, 50**
deposcit (deposco)	demands, beseeches	**52**
deposuit (depono)	laid, deposited	**20, 26**
descendo, descendi	descend, sink, decline	**38**
desideratissimus, -a, -um	most mourned, longed after	48
desideratus, -a, -um	yearned after, missed	39
desiderium, -ii	object of desire, grief for loss	**23, 42**
Deus, -i	God	*10*
devotus, -a, -um	devoted	40
dicam (dico)	I might tell	**37**

dictus, -a, -um	(afore)said	**28, 33**
die (dies)	(on) the day	**1, 3**
dieb(us) (dies)	days	**5**
diem (dies)	day	**24**
dies, diei	day	**41**
difficilis, -e	difficult, dangerous	**29**
dignissimus, -a, -um	most worthy	
dignus, -a, -um	worthy, deserving	24
dilectissimus, -a, -um	most beloved	33, **35**, 39
dilectus, -a, -um	beloved	
discendentis (descendo)	fading, declining	**38**
discessit (discedo)	departed	**39**
dissolutio, -tionem	death, dissolution	50
diu	for a long time	
diurnant (diurno)	they last long	52
diutinus, -a, -um	long-lasting, chronic	**41**
diutissime	for a very long time, for ever	43
diuturnus, -a, -um	long-lasting, lengthy	37
diversus, -a, -um	various	
dividendus, -a, -um (divido)	to be separated	**50**
divinus, -a, -um	of God	
dni *vide* dominus	of the Lord	8
do, dedi	give	
doctor, -oris	doctor	31
doctrina, -ae	doctrine, learning, belief	30, 42
doctus, -a, -um	learned, skilled	51
dolor, doloris	sorrow	30, 48
domina, -ae	lady	**4**
Dom(ini)	of the Lord	**1**
Domino	Lord	**21**
dominus, -i	lord	4, 18, 47
donum, -i	gift	**44**
dormio, dormivi	sleep	10, 11
dos, dotis	gift, quality	
doto, dotavi	endow	
dotibus (dos)	with gifts, endowments	52
dti *vide* dictus	(afore)said	33
dubius, -a, -um	doubtful, uncertain	
ducis (dux)	of the duke	
duco, duxi	lead, lead to marriage	

dulcis, -e	sweet, beloved	
dum	while	52
duo, duae	two	**50**
duobus (duo)	two (*ablative*)	**17**
duodecim	twelve	
duodecimus, -a, -um	twelfth	
durissime	most firmly, harshly	
durus, -a, -um	hard	51
dux, ducis	leader, duke	
e	out of	**8**, 30
ea (is)	she, her	**49**
eadem (idem)	the same	44
earum (is)	of them	
ecce	behold	
ecclesia, -ae	church	5
edax, edacis	devourer	
efflavit (efflo)	breathed forth	**21**
efflo, efflavi	breathe forth	**21**
egenus, -a, -um	poor, needy	45
ego	I	**26**
egregie	excellently, admirably	
egregius, -a, -um	distinguished, excellent, admirable	23, 42
eius (is)	his, hers, its	8, 28
eiusdem (idem)	of the same	**5**, 48
ejus *vide* eius	his, hers, its	**3, 18, 50**
ejusdem *vide* eiusdem	of the same	39, 44, 46
elegans, elegantis	elegant	
elegantia, -ae	elegance, grace	24
elegit (eligo)	chose	**49**
eligo, eligi	choose	**49**
eloquium, -ii	speech, eloquence	51
enim	truly, indeed	52
eodem (idem)	the same	**10**
eorum (is)	of them, their	45
epi(scopus), -i	bishop	31
eques, equitis	knight	**4**
eram (sum)	I was	**26**
erat (sum)	he/she/it was	**26**, 51

erexit (erigo)	erected, set up	46
erga	towards	44
ergo	therefore	33
eruditissimus, -a, -um	most learned	
eruditus, -a, -um	learned, erudite	
es (sum)	thou art	**23**
est (sum)	is	*5*
et	and	*2*
et ... et	both ... and	**44**
eternus, etc. *vide* aeternus	eternal	7,21
etiam	also, still, certainly	*8*
eum (is)	him	44
eundem (idem)	the same	40
ex	from, out of	**11, 33**
excelsus, -a, -um	high	47
excessit (excedo)	went forth, departed	
excitaverat (excito)	had aroused	**48**
excolo, excolui	cultivate	**47**
excultus, -a, -um	cultivated, ennobled	**44**
executor, -oris	executor	
exemplar, -aris	copy, model, example	
exemplum, -i	example, pattern	43, 44
exequias *vide* exsequiae	funeral ceremony	**52**
exerceo, exercui	practise, work at	**35**
exercuit	practised	**35**
exeuntis, -e (exeo)	passing away, departing	**15**
exhalo, -avi	breathe forth	
eximie	remarkably	
eximius, -a, -um	remarkable, extraordinary, exceptional	43
exitus, -us	issue, a going out	**28**
exorno, exornavi	furnish with, adorn	
expectandae (exspecto)	to be longed for	38
expectans, -antis (exspecto)	awaiting, hoping for, etc.	**21**, 50
exsequiae, -arum	funeral procession, funeral ceremony	**52**
exspecto, -avi	hope for, long for, await	**34**
extremus, -a, -um	final	
exuviae, -arum	(mortal) remains	**20,** 26

facilis, -e	easy, kind	
factus, -a, -um (facio)	made	34
facundus, -a, -um	eloquent	31
faecibus (faex)	dregs	**51**
faelix *vide* felix	fortunate	51, **52**
faemina *vide* femina	woman	49
faex, faecis	dregs, refuse	**51**
fama, -æ	fame	
familia, -ae	family	21, 52
familiaris, -e	familiar, of the same family	
fatum, -i	fate, destiny, destruction	**37**
fecit (facio)	made	**46**
felicissimus, -a, -um	most fortunate, joyous	7
feliciter	happily, joyously, successfully	11, 35, 47
felix, felicis	fortunate, lucky, joyous	51, **52**
femina, -ae	woman	49
fenestra, -ae	window	23
fere	nearly	37
ferme	almost, very nearly	**24**
festinus, -a, -um	hurrying, hasty	52
fidelis, -e	faithful	45, 49
fidelitas, -litatis	loyalty, faithfulness	18, 24
fideliter	faithfully	
fides, fidei	faith	36, **49**
fidessimus, -a, -um	most faithful	40
filia, -ae	daughter	**2, 16**
filibus (filius)	children *(ablative plural)*	37
filii, filiorum	children, sons	**43, 48**
filii(que) (filius)	son	**5**
filiolus, -i	little son	37
filius, filii	son	**16, 30**
firmus, -a, -um	firm, strong	20
fit (fio)	is made, is done	**28**
flagrantis, -e	blazing, burning	
flebilior, -oris	more grief-stricken	**24**
flebilis, -e	causing grief, wept for, mourned by	**19, 24**, 47

floruit	flourished	
flos, floris	flower	**26**
forma, -ae	form, shape, beauty	24
formosissimus, -a, -um	most beautiful	50
fortiter	strongly, stoutly, bravely	13
fractus, -a, -um	weakened, broken	
frater, fratris	brother	*10*
frigidum *vide* frigidus	cold	44
frigidus, -a, -um	cold	44
fructuosus, -a, -um	fruitful, profitable	
fructus, -us	fruit, profit	52
frugifer, -fera, -ferum	fruitful, fertile, profitable	47
frui (fruor)	enjoy	
frustra	in vain	
fuerunt (sum)	have been, were	**22**
fugiens, -ientis (fugio)	departing, taking flight	**50**
fuisse (sum)	to have been	**44**
fuisti (sum)	thou wert	51
fuit (sum)	was	**9**
funera (funus)	death	**9**
funestus, -a, -um	fatal	
funus, funeris	death, funeral	**9**
futurus, -a, -um (sum)	about to be, future	**20**, 49, 52
gaudium, -ii	joy, gladness	**51**
gen *vide* generosus	Gentleman	**2**
generalis, -e	general	13
generis (genus)	family	**50**
generosus, -i	Gentleman	**2**
genius, -ii	talent, genius, intellect	30
gens, gentis	people, family, clan	**47**
genus, generis	race, kind, sort, genus	**50**, 51, 52
gloria, -ae	glory	
gradum, -i	step, degree	
grammaticalis, -e	grammar (school)	45
grate	freely	
gratiâ	by grace	
gratiae	thanks	
gratissime	most pleasantly	
gubernator, -oris	governor	**8**, **28**, 45

habeant (habeo)	have	**24**
habemus (habeo)	we have	49
habeo, habui	have	49
habes (habeo)	thou hast	**51**
hac (hic)	this	**11**, 50
hâc (hic)	in this (way)	
haec (hic)	this, the latter	**18**, 29
haereo, haesi	cling to, adhere	51
haeres, haeredis *vide* heres	heir	**49**
haeret (haereo)	clings to	51
hanc (hic)	this	*6*
haud	not, by no means	38, 49
haudquaquam	by no means, not at all	45
heic *vide* hic	here	**16**, 31
heres, heredis	heir	**28**, 49
heu	alas	36
hic	here	**2, 3**
hic, haec, hoc	this, the latter	**48**
hiems, hiemis	winter	37
hinc	hence	
hoc (hic)	this	**10**
homo, hominis	man	**36**
honestissimus, -a, -um	most honourable	47
honestus, -a, -um	graceful, honourable	
honor, honoris	honour, dignity, respect	
honoratus, -a, -um	honoured, distinguished	34
hosp(itium, -ii)	inn, lodging	**52**
huic (hic)	to this	**19**, 24
huius (hic)	of this	**5**
huiusce	of this (*emphatic*)	**8**
hujus *vide* huius	of this	*7*
hujusce *vide* huiusce	of this (*emphatic*)	**39**
humanitate (humanitas)	by courtesy, kindness	
humanus, -a, -um	human	
humilis, -e	humble, low, poor	45
humus, -i	earth, soil	26
hunc (hic)	this	13, 20, 39
hyacynthus, -i	hyacinth	52
hyeme *vide* hiems	winter	**37**

iacent (iaceo)	they lie	
iacet (iaceo)	lies	**2**
iam	now	
iamdudum	now for a long time	**22**
ibi	there	
ibidem	in the same place	
idem	the same	
identidem	now and then	
Id(us, Iduum)	Ides	**19**
ignarus, -a, -um	ignorant, inexperienced	45
illa (ille)	that one, she	**11**
ille, illa, illud	that one	**11, 18, 37**
ille, illa	the former	**29, 48**
illic	there	37
illius (ille)	of him	
illorum (ille)	of them	**29**
illustro, -avi	illustrate, explain	43
immaturus, -a, -um	untimely	42, 52
immemor, -oris	unmindful	**38**
immensus, -a, -um	boundless	
immortalis, -e	immortal	**26**, 29
in	in, into	**6, 11**
inanis, -e	empty, void	
incertus, -a, -um	uncertain	12
inchoaverunt (inchoo)	they began, started	**29**
inclytus, -a, -um	celebrated, renowned	
incola, -ae	inhabitant	40
incorporatus, -a, -um	incorporated	28
incorruptus, -a, -um	sound, perfect, pure	
incubuit (incumbo)	brooded over, studied	
inculcatus, -a, -us	inculcated	44
inculpatus, -a, -um	blameless	**49**
indignus, -a, -um	unworthy	45
indoles, -is	nature, natural disposition	47
infandus, -a, -um	unspeakable, shocking	
infelicis, -e	unhappy	
ingeniosus, -a, -um	talented	
ingenium, -ii	talent, cleverness	*40*
ingens, ingentis	immense, enormous	48
ingravescentes	aggravating, rendering worse	**41**

inhumatur	is buried	
inhumatus, -a, -um (inhumo)	buried	38
inimicus, -i	enemy	**13**
inquirimus (inquiro)	we seek, look for	49
insero, inserui	place, set in place	**26**
insigniverit (insignio)	adorned, distinguished	
insignus, -a, -um	remarkable, extraordinary	41
insula, -ae	island	19
insuper	in addition, besides	17
integerrimus, -a, -um	virtuous, upright	40, 43
intemeratus, -a, -um	unspotted, undefiled	**49**
interim	meanwhile	
intra	within	
intumulatus, -a, -um	interred	
invenient (invenio)	they will find	**36**
invenio, inveni	find	**11, 34**, 39
invidus, -a, -um	envious	**32**
invitus, -a, -um	unwilling, against one's will	37
ipse, ipsa, ipsum	him/her/itself	29, **38**, 49
ipsius (ipse)	of the same, of himself, etc.	**25**, 52
ipsorum (ipse)	of the same	
irrorate (irroro)	moisten, sprinkle with dew	**52**
iste, ista, istud	that same, that particular	**26**, 43
ita *vide* ut...ita	so	**6**
iucundissimus, -a, -um	very pleasant, agreeable	
iudex, iudicis	judge, magistrate	34
iudicium, -ii	judgement, understanding, opinion	40
iusticiarius, -ii	judge, justice	34
iustissimus, -a, -um	most just, impartial	
iustitia, -ae	justice	34
iuvenis, -is	youth, young person	48, 52
iuxta	next to	*13*
iuxtim	near, close by	38
jacent *vide* iacent	they lie	
jacet *vide* iacet	lies	**3**
jacit *vide* iacet	lies	**7**
jamdudum *vide* iamdudum	now for a long time	**22**

jucundissimam		
vide iucundissimus	very pleasant, agreeable	
judicium *vide* iudicium	judgement	40
juvenis *vide* iuvenis	young man	42
juxta *vide* iuxta	next to, nearby	
juxtim *vide* iuxtim	near, close by	38
kalendae, -arum	Kalends, the first day of the month	**5**
karissima *vide* carissimus	dearest	**5**
labor, laboris	labour, struggle, endeavour	**34**
laborans, -antis	working, toiling, struggling	50
lachrimula, -ae	little tear	52
lachrymas *vide* lacrima	tears	52
lacrima, -ae	tear	52
laete	joyfully, gladly	
laetus, -a, -um	joyful, glad	51
languens, -entis (langueo)	languishing	37
lapis, lapidis	stone, marble	**38**, 39
laudabitur (laudo)	shall be praised	49
laus, laudis	praise	28
lautus, -a, -um	elegant	
lectissimus, -a, -um	most excellent	48, 49
lector, -toris	reader	24, 52
lege (lego)	read (*imperative*)	45
lego, legi	read	
legum (lex)	of laws	**40**
lex, legis	law	**40**
libate (libo)	offer, pour in libation	**52**
libens, -entis	willing, glad	37
liberalis, -e	gentlemanly, generous	
libere	freely	
liberi, liberorum	children	**19**
lilium, -ii	lily	52
literae, -arum	letters	**47**
literarum (literae)	of letters	
literatus, -a, -um	learned	
locus, -i	place	13
longe	at length	
longus, -a, -um	long	23, **33**

lubens *vide* libens	willing, glad, sacrificing	**37**
luctuo *vide* luctuosus	lamentable	**37**
luctuosissimus, -a, -um	most grieving, sorrowing	41
luctuosus, -a, -um	lamentable	**37**
ludus, -i	game, school	
lugens, lugentis	sorrowing, lamenting	37
luget (lugeo)	bewails, laments	36
lugete (lugeo)	weep ye	**52**
lux, lucis	light	
maerens, -entis (maereo)	mourning, grieving	33
maestissimus, -a, -um	most grieving	**48**
magis	more	
magister, -tri	master	**12**
magnanimus, -a, -um	high-minded, courageous	13
magnopere	exceedingly	
magnus, -a, -um	great	21, 23
maiores, maiorum	ancestors, forefathers	**23**, 46
majores, majorum		
vide maiores	ancestors, forefathers	**23**, 46
mala (malus)	evils	
manens, manentis (maneo)	remaining, continuing, lasting	**49**
manufactus, -a, -um	made by hand, by man	**49**
marito, maritavi	marry	**52**
maritus, -i	husband	*29*
marmor, marmoris	marble, stone	**10**
mater, matris	mother	49
maximus, -a, -um	greatest, eldest	**2**, 5
me	me	26
medicinae	of medicine	
medicus, -a, -um	medicinal	**35**, 37
medicus, -i	physician, doctor	
melior, melius	better	**11**
mellitissimus, -a, -um	most delightful	52
memento (memini)	remember	**38**
memor, memoris	mindful	35
memorandus, -a, -um		
(memoro)	to be remembered	25
memoria, -ae	memory	**4, 18, 34**
memoris	memory	**49**

mens, mentis	mind, reason, intellect, soul	**51**
mensis, mensis	month	**5**, 13, 23
mentibus (mens)	to souls	51
mentis (mens)	of mind	**51**
mercator, -toris	merchant	9, **17**, 49
mercedes (merces)	reward	
meritissime	most deservedly	48
meritu *vide* meritum	by merit	**34**
meritum, -i	merit	**34**
meruit (mereo)	deserved, merited	**48**
migravo, migravi	travel	
mihi	to me	**23**, 51
miles, militis	knight, soldier	**9**
minime	not at all, in the least degree	**45**
minor, minoris	less, younger	**48**
minus	less	**20**, 46
misereatur (misereor)	may (he) have mercy on	**10**
misericordia, -æ	mercy	21
mitis, mite	gentle, meek	
modestus, -a, -um	temperate, discreet	
modus, -i	measure, mean, limit	**42**, 50
moerens, -entis *vide* maerens	mourning	**12**
moestissimus, etc.		
vide maestissimus	most grieving	**48**
molestus, -a, -um	burdensome, troublesome	45
monumentum, -i	monument	**41**
morbosus, -a, -um	ill	
morbus, -i	disease, illness	37, **41**, 51
mores, morum (mos)	character, manners, disposition	*40*
mori (morior)	to die	12, **38**
moribundus, -a, -um	dying	
moribus (mos)	by manners, character	42, 44, 47
mors, mortis	death	42, 50, **51**
mortalis, -e	mortal	**10, 26, 32**
mortalitas, -tatis	mortality	35
morte (mors)	by death	*7*
mortem (mors)	death	**39**
morti (mors)	to death	**12**, 13
mortuus, -a, -um	dead	**31**, 39
morum (mores)	of nature, character, disposition	24

mos, moris	nature, character, disposition	40
mulier, mulieris	woman	49
multus, -a, -um	many	**6**
mundus, -i	world	
munificus, -a, -um	liberal, bounteous	45
munus, muneris	gift	
Musae, -arum	Muses	52
musica, -ae	music	
nata, -ae	born, daughter	**14, 33, 50**
natu	by birth	**2**
natura, -ae	nature, disposition, character	52
natus, -a, -um	born	**26**
natus, nata	aged	**24**
ne	not, lest	**26, 37**
nec	and indeed not	**26**
nec...nec	neither...nor	**45**
nec non *vide* necnon	and also	**25**
necesse	necessary	24
necnon	and also	*15*
nepos, nepotis	grandson, nephew	**16, 38**
nihil	nothing	
nimirum	certainly, undoubtedly	52
nimius, -a, -um	too much, too great	52
nisi	if not, unless	
nitor, nitoris	brightness, splendour	
niveus, -a, -um	snowy, white as snow	**52**
nobilissimus, -a, -um	most noble	47
nomen, nominis	name	48
nomini	by renown	
non	not	**38**
Non(ae), Nonarum	Nones	41
nonus, -a, -um	ninth	
norma, -ae	pattern, model	**52**
noster, nostra, nostrum	our	21
nota, -ae	note, sign	49
novem	nine	35, 49
novo *vide* nonus	ninth	**28**
novus, -a, -um	new	
nullus, -a, -um	none	**25, 40**

numerosus, -a, -um	many, copious	
numquam	never	**49**
nunc	now	33
nunquam *vide* numquam	never	**49**
nuper	lately, not long ago	18, 33, 40
nuperrime	very recently	**22**
nuptus, -a, -um (nubo)	married	
ob	for, on account of	46
ob *vide* obiit	died	**6**
obdormio, -ivi	fall asleep (in death)	**6**
obdormiverunt (obdormio)	fell asleep	**18**
obeo, obii (obivi)	go to, meet (death)	
obierunt (obeo)	they died	32
ob(ii)t (obeo)	died	**1, 24, 39**
obijt *vide* obiit	died	**2**
obitus, -us	death	
obivit *vide* obiit	died	37
occido, occidi	die	**19, 24**
occubo, occubui	rest in the grave, succumb	**12**
octavus, -a, -um	eighth	13, 26
octo	eight	39, 43
octodecimus. -a, -um	eighteenth	**10**
octogenarius, -i	octogenarian	20, 38
octoginta	eighty	39
officio	by kindness	
officium, -ii	office, service, duty	**18**
olim	formerly, once upon a time	**22**
omnes (omnis)	all	23, **40**
omnibus (omnis)	by all, to all (men)	43, 45
omnino	entirely	40
omnis, omne	all	51
omnium (omnis)	of all (men)	21, 30
opera (opus)	works	
opis (ops)	resources	**37**
oppidum, -i	town	45
oppugnando (oppugno)	in attacking	**13**
ops, opis	resources, assistance	**37**
optime (bene)	thoroughly, excellently	48
optimus, -a, -um (bonus)	best	**51**

orator, oratoris	speaker	
oriundus, -a, -um	sprung from, born of	**33**
ornatissimus, -a, -um	highly distinguished	52
ornatus, -a, -um	honoured, distinguished, respected	21
orno, ornavi	honour, distinguish, adorn	47
ortus, -a, -um	born, risen	21, 47
ossa (os)	bones	
otium, -ii	ease	
pace (pax)	in peace	**6,** 34, 36
pacem (pax)	peace	34
pacis (pax)	of peace	19
paene	nearly, almost	
par, paris	equal to, like	36, 52
parcite (parco)	spare, refrain from injuring	**32**
parens, parentis	parent	43
parentu(m) *vide* parens	of parents	**37**
paries, parietis	wall	20
pariter	in like manner, also	
par(ochia, -ae)	parish	**19**
parochialis, -e	parish (*adj.*)	
pars, partis	part	**49**
partibus (pars)	by parts, in parts	**6**
parturiens (parturio)	giving birth	**49**
pastor, pastoris	pastor, minister, shepherd	5, 43
pater, patris	father	
paternitas, -tatis	fatherhood	**45**
paternus, -a, -um	paternal	
patiens, -entis	patient, able to bear	
patientia, -ae	patience, endurance	41
patre (pater)	from a father	29
patris (pater)	of a father	33
patrius, -a, -um	of the fatherland, native, national	13, 47
paucus, -a, -um	few, little	
pax, pacis	peace	
pene *vide* paene	nearly, almost	**20**
peperit (pario)	brought forth, bore (children)	**49**
per	for, by, through	35, 43

peractus, -a, -um (perago)	accomplished, completed	**18, 29, 39**
perantiquus, -a, -um	ancient	
perennaret (perenno)	might last many years	**52**
perennis, -e	lasting, durable, perennial	
perillustris, -e	very evident, highly distinguished	52
peritus, -a, -um	expert, skilful	35
perpetuus, -a, -um	perpetual	
perpolitus, -a, -um	polished, accomplished	52
pessimus, -a, -um (malus)	worst	**51**
pharmacapola		
vide pharmacopola	pharmacist, chemist	45
pharmacopola	pharmacist, chemist	45
piae (pius)	pious	**18**
piam (pius)	pious	46
pientissimus, -a, -um (piens)	most pious, affectionate	**43**
pietas, pietatis	piety, compassion	*18*
piissimus, -a, -um (pius)	most pious	50
pius, -a, -um	pious, affectionate	
placide	quietly	18
placidus, -a, -um	quiet, still, placid	**21**
plenus, -a, -um	full	**21**
plures	several	
plus, pluris	more	**20**, 46
ponendum (pono)	to be placed	**10,** 39
poni (pono)	to be placed	23, 38
pono, posui	place	
positus, -a, -um (pono)	placed, laid	26
possem (possum)	I might	**26**
possint (possum)	they may	44
post	after	9, 18, 50
post	beneath	**25**
postea	afterwards	
posteri, posterorum	posterity	**32**, 52
posthac	after this, hereafter	26
postquam	after, after that, as soon as	
posuerunt (pono)	they placed	43
posuit (pono)	(he) placed	**6, 41**
praebendarius, -ii	prebendary	43
praecentor, -oris	precentor	30

praeceptum, -i	precept, command, injunction	43
praecharissimus, -a, -um	most dearly beloved	**27**
praecipuae	especially	
praecipue	especially	
praecox, praecocis	ripe before time, immature	52
praedictus, -a, -um	aforesaid	26, 35
praeditus, -a, -um	endowed with	
praeeuntium (praeeo)	departed, gone before	35
praefectus, -i	commander, governor	15
Praeficae, -arum	Præficæ, mourners	**52**
praenobilis, -e	very famous, celebrated	4
praeparo, praeparavi	prepare, make ready	
praeproperus, -a, -um	over-hasty, impatient	11
praereptus, -a, -um (praeripio)	plucked, snatched away	**52**
praestabat (praesto)	excelled	
praestans, -stantis	excellent, distinguished	42
praestes (praesto)	you show (respect)	**24**
praeter	besides, except	
praetor, praetoris	mayor, chief magistrate	**18**
preparatam *vide* praeparo	prepared	50
presbytero (presbyter)	to (the) priest	**14**
prid(ie)	the day before	**5**, 41
primogenitus, -a, -um	firstborn	11, 31
primus, -a, -um	first	**8**, 28, 49
princeps, principis	prince	
priscus, -a, -um	old-fashioned, ancient, stern	**36**
privatus, -a, -um	private	
pro	for, on behalf of	7, 43, 44
proavus, -i	great-grandfather, ancestor	**22**, 23
probatus, -a, -um	pleasant, excellent	
probe	honestly, rightly	
probitas, probitatis	uprightness, probity, honesty	43
probus, -a, -um	upright, honest	35
professor, -oris	professor, doctor (academic)	**30**
profundus, -a, -um	profound, high	
proles, prolis	offspring, issue	**10**
pronepos, -nepotis	great-grandson	
prope	near, close by	**2**
propinquus, -i	neighbour	**19**
proprius, -a, -um	one's own	**6**

propter	owing to, on account of	
prorsus	in a word, to sum up	43
prosapia, -ae	race, lineage, family	
prosecuti sunt (prosequor)	accompanied, honoured	40
providae	caring, prudent, provident	**49**
prudens, prudentis	prudent, wise, practical	**49**
prudentia, -ae	wisdom, discretion	**52**
publicus, -a, -um	public, common	**13**
pudor, pudoris	shame	**42**
puer, pueri	boy	
pueritia, pueritiæ	boyhood	52
pulvis, pulveris	dust	
qua	which, who, to what extent	44
quadraginta	forty	
quae (qui)	who, which	**3, 29**
quamthan,	how much	24, **36**, 50
quam (qui)	which, whom	**35, 36**
quando	when, at what time	12
quantus, -a, -um	how much	37
quartus, -a, -um	fourth	39
quasi	about, as if	46
quatuor	four	**8**, 50
quatuordecim	fourteen	
-que	and	**5, 7, 26**
que (quis)	who	**48**
quem (qui)	whom	**40**, 42
qui, quae, quod	who	**6, 11, 18**
quibus (quis)	whose, to whom	**28**, 48, 52
quicquid (quisquis)	whatever	**10**
quicunque	whoever	
quid (quis)	any	24
quid ni?	why not?	
quidam	a certain	28
quidem	indeed, truly	44
quiesco, quievi	rest	
quiescunt (quiesco)	they rest	45
quiete	quietly, silently	
quin	but	
quindecim	fifteen	

quinquaginta	fifty	
quinque	five	50
quintus, -a, -um	fifth	21, 45
quis	what	**42**
quo (qui)	by which, in which	21
quod (quis)	that, what	**44**
quondam	once, formerly	34, 46
quoque	also	**10**
quorum (quis)	of which	
quotquot	as many as	
quum	when	
raptus, -a, -um (rapto)	snatched, abducted	**11**
raro	seldom, rarely	52
ratio, rationis	reason, intelligence	
recessit (recedo)	departed, died	**10**
recidam (recido)	I may fall	**26**
recondo, -didi	laid aside, hid	
rector, rectoris	ruler, rector	**5**
reddidit (reddo)	gave back	49, 50
regalis, -e	royal	19
regius, -a, -um	royal	
regnans, regnantis	reigning	
regnum, -i	monarchy	23
rei familiari	property	
rei-medicae	(of) medical matters	**35**
relictus, -a, -um	left behind, relict	**37**
religio, religionis	devotion, piety, conscience	44
relinquens, -entis (relinquo)	leaving behind	43
relinquo, reliqui	leave behind	
reliqui, -orum	the rest	**44**
reliquiae, -arum	remains	*13*
reliquit (relinquo)	left behind	**17**
rependere (rependo)	repay, recompense	44
repositus, -a, -um	placed, buried	37
reputatus, -a, -um	reckoned, considered	
requies, requietis	rest, a resting place	34, 39
requiescat (requiesco)	may he/she rest	**6**, 36
requiescit (requiesco)	he/she rests	**2**
requiesco, requievi	rest, sleep, repose	

rerum (res)	of things	
res, rei	thing, matter, affair	35
residentiarius, -a, -um	in residence	30, 31
resigno, -avi	resign, leave	
restituo, -ui	restore	**6**
resurrectio, -tionis	resurrection	**10**
revera	truly, indeed	25
reverendus, -a, -um	revered, respected	**6**
reverentia, -ae	reverence, respect	24
Revi *vide* reverendus	Reverend	**39**
rex, regis	king	
sacer, sacra, sacrum	sacred, holy	**4, 6**
saeculum, -i	the age, the times	52
sagax, sagacis	shrewd, wise	
salus, salutis	salvation, health, safety	**12**
salvator, -toris	saviour	**36**
salve	welcome, hail	51
sanctus, -a, -um	holy	**30**
sanctus, sancta	saint	**43**
sanus, -a, -um	healthy, sound, sane, sensible	40
satur, satura, saturum	full	
schola, -ae	school	42, 45
scientia, -ae	knowledge, science, philosophy	47
scripta (scriptum)	writings	40
sct *vide* sanctus	saint	**43**
se	himself, herself, itself	**13**
secundus, -a, -um	second, following	**3, 40, 49**
sed	but	**26**, 36, **49**
sedecim	sixteen	
sedes, sedis	seat, grave, spot	**50**
semel	once	
semper	always	
senectus, -tutis	old age	
senilis, -e	of an old man, senile, mature	**52**
septem	seven	
septemdecim	seventeen	
septemdecimus, -a, -um	seventeenth	**8**
septimus, -a, -um	seventh	**22**, 38
septuagesimus, -a, -um	seventieth	7

septuaginta	seventy	**39**
sepulchralis, -e	of a tomb, sepulchral	38
sepulchrum, -i	tomb, sepulchre	10, 45
sepultus, -a, -um (sepelio)	buried	**5, 46**
series, series	series, succession, lineage	23
servus, -i	servant	**19**
sex	six	
sexagesimus, -a, -um	sixtieth	
sexaginta	sixty	
sextus, -a, -um	sixth	**3, 7**
si	if	24
sibi (se)	himself, etc. *(dative)*	45
sic	so, in this manner	**26**
sicut	as, just as	23
simul	at the same time	**18**, 40
sincerus, -a, -um	sound, honest,sincere	40
sine	without	**10, 28**
singularis, -e	singular, excellent, extraordinary	40
sint (sum)	they may be	**24**
siste (sisto)	stand still, pause *(imperative)*	
sit (sum)	may be	**42**
sitiens, -entis (sitio)	thirsting after, eagerly desiring	**32**
situs, -a, -um (sino)	buried, placed	**5**, 16, 31
soboles *vide* suboles	offspring	52
socius, -ii	friend, fellow (of college), partner	**19**, 45
solebant (soleo)	were accustomed	46
solenniter	solemnly, customarily	46
solum, -i	soil, earth	44
sopultus *vide* sepultus	buried	**46**
soror, sororis	sister	**12**
sors, sortis	rank, fate, fortune	**45**
spe (spes)	in hope	**10**
spectator, -oris	spectator	45
spectatus, -a, -um	seen, remarkable	
sperans, sperantis (spero)	hoping, trusting	44
speratus, -a, -um (spero)	hoped for	52
spes, spei	hope	48, 47
spiritus, -us	spirit, breath, soul	26
stae *vide* sanctus	saint	**19**

stemmate (stemma)	family tree, lineage	33
stipendia	salaries	
stirps, stirpis	stock, trunk, family	21, 47
strenue	bravely	
strenuus, -a, -um	brave	
studia, studiorum	studies	
sua (suus)	his, hers	40, 50
suae (suus)	his, hers	**1, 47**
suam (suus)	his, hers	20, 50
suas (suus)	his, hers	20
suavissimus, -a, -um	sweetest	47
suavitas, -itatis	sweetness, pleasantness	24, 43
suaviter	sweetly	
sub	under	14, **50**
subito	suddenly	
subitus, -a, -um	unexpected, sudden	**39**
suboles, subolis	offspring, issue	52
subter	beneath, below	10, 35, 45
subtilis, -e	fine, acute, subtle	30
subtus	below, beneath	
succubuit (succumbo)	succumbed to	**13**
sufficeret (sufficio)	might suffice	
sufficiente (sufficio)	providing	41
sufficio, suffeci	supply, provide, suffice	
sui (se)	of himself, etc.	**43**
sui (suus)	his, etc., own (family, friends)	**40**, 50
sui (suus)	of his, etc.	48
suis (suus)	by his, to his, etc.	**29**, 50
summus, -a, -um	highest, greatest	18, 48, 51
sumo *vide* summus	highest, greatest	**34**
sumptus, -us	cost, expense	**6**
sunt (sum)	are	16, 26, 35
suo (suus)	by his, etc.	52
suorum (suus)	of his, etc., (family)	**48**
superstes, -stitis	surviving	
supersum, superfui	remain, are left behind	
supersunt *vide* supersum	are remaining	50
supplex, supplicis	humble	45
supradictus, -a, -um	above-mentioned	**10**, 13
supremus, -a, -um	final, last	**24**

surculus, -i	sprout, shoot	52
surgere (surgo)	to rise from sleep	26
susceperit (suscipio)	had received	
suscipio, suscepi	receive, suffer, endure	
sustineo, sustinui	sustain, support	**41**
sustulit (suffero, tollo)	endured, suffered, took away	**51**
suus, sua, suum	his, hers, its (own)	
tabes, tabis	wasting away, consumption	47
talis, -e	of such a special kind	52
tam	such, so	**42**
tam...quam	as...as	**50**
tamen	however	
tandem	at length, at last	
tantus, -a, -um	so many, so much	
tardus, -a, -um	slow	36
te	you (thee)	36
tectus, -a, -um (tego)	covered	**26**
tego, texi	cover (with earth), bury	**51**
tem *vide* tum	also	**40**
templum, -i	temple	46
tempora (tempus)	times	51
tempus, temporis	time	
tenebrae, -arum	darkness, gloom	
tenens, tenentis (teneo)	holding, preserving	**24**
tenentur (teneo)	are held, gripped	**40**
tener, tenera, tenerum	tender, youthful	
terra, -ae	land, earth	51
terrae, -arum (terra)	the world	**7**
terris (terrae)	(in) the world	**7**
tertius, -a, -um	third	**8, 43**, 52
testamentus, -i	last will, testament	48
testamonium,		
vide testimonium	testimony, witness	**21**
testantur (testor)	they bear witness, testify	**40**
testimonium, -i	testimony, witness	**21**
theologia, -ae	divinity, theology	**30**, 31
thesaurarius, -ii	treasurer	**30**, 31
thesaurus, -i	treasure	31
timens, timentis (timeo)	fearing	49

tot	so many	44
totidem(que)	(and) just as many	**17**
totius (totus)	of all	**15**
totus, -a, -um	all, whole	37
trado, tradidi	recommend, deliver	43
tranquille	quietly, peacefully	39
transegisset (transigo)	might accomplish	**37**
transmigrarunt (transmigro)	made a journey, migrated	**11**
tredecim	thirteen	
tres	three	17
tricesimus, -a, -um	thirtieth	
triginta	thirty	
trimestris, -e	three months old	**11**
triste	sadly	
tu	you (thou)	51
tua (tuus)	your (thy)	51
tum	then, as well	
tumulatus, -a, -um	buried	
tumulus, -i	tomb, burial mound	11
tutissimus, -a, -um	safest	**11**
tuus, tua, tuum	your (thy)	36
ubi	where	36
ubique	everywhere	
ullus, -a, -um	any	
ultimus, -a, -um	last, furthest, final	37
umquam	ever	
una cum	together with	**16**
unde	whence, from where	26
undecim	eleven	
undecimus, -a, -um	eleventh	**10**
undetricesimus, -a, -um	twenty-ninth	**12, 39**
unicus, -a, -um	only, unparalled	13, **20, 37**
unius (unus)	of one, one of	**37**
unquam *vide* umquam	ever	**36**
unus, -a, -um	one	**8**, 30, 39
urbanus, -a, -um	pleasant, agreeable, urbane	
urbs, urbis	city	49
urna, -ae	urn	51
usque ad	until	38

usus, -a, -um	used	
ut	so that	**26,** 52
ut...ita	as...so	**6**
uterque, utraque, utrumque	each of two	**16**
utpote	inasmuch as	
utriusque (uterque)	of each of two	**16**
uxor, uxoris	wife	**2, 3**
vale	farewell	51
valedico, valedixi	say farewell	
valetudo, -inis	health	
valuit (valeo)	was strong, was able	
varius, -a, -um	many, manifold, various	**18**
vecors, vecordis	mad, insane, foolish	**38**
vel	or, especially	52
velum, -i	cover	14
venerabilis, -e	venerable	
venerari (veneror)	to worship	**46**
veneratio, -tionis	reverence, respect	40
veniens, -ientis (venio)	coming	**51**
venio, veni	come	
verbus, -i	word	
vere	truly	
vernans, -nantis	springing, flourishing	**52**
vernus, -i	spring(time)	**26**
vero	indeed, only, although	**36,** 48
viator, -oris	passer-by, traveller	
vicarius, -ii	vicar	**38**
vicecomes, -comitis	viscount	52
vices(s)imus, -a, -um	twentieth	13, 45, 52
vicus, -i	village	40
vid(elicet)	videlicet, namely	**46**
vidua, -ae	widow	4, 43
viduus, -i	widower	50
vigens, vigentis	flourishing, thriving	
vigesimus, -a, -um	twentieth	**8**
vigilantia, -ae	watchfulness, vigilance	
viginti	twenty	8, 20, 24
vim (vis)	power, strength, force	40
vindex, vindicis	defender, protector, guardian	40

vir, viri	man	**6**, 35, 45
vires, -ium (vis)	strength	**41**
virgo, virginis	virgin, maid	14
virtus, virtutis	worth, excellence, virtue	**9**
virtutes (virtus)	courage	47
vis	power, strength, force	40
vita, -ae	life	**11, 49**
vitreus, -a, -um	made of glass	23
vivens, entis (vivo)	living	**17, 50**
vivere (vivo)	to live	25
vivit (vivo)	lives	**9**
vivo, vixit	live	
vivus, -a, -um	living	**31**, 40, **51**
vix	scarcely	
vixisset (vivo)	might have lived	**49**
vixit (vivo)	lived	5, 10, 21
viz (videlicet)	that is	**30**
vobis (vos)	to you	**32**
vocans, vocantis (voco)	calling, summoning	**10**
voce (vox)	by voice	44
volens, volentis (volo)	willing	**50**
voluntas, voluntatis	will	
vos	you	52
vulgaris, -e	common, ordinary	49

Some Initials and Abbreviations

A.B.		**5**
Artium Baccalaureus	Bachelor of Arts	
A.C.		41
Anno Christi	In the year of Christ	
Æræ Christianæ ·	Of the Christian Era	
A.D.		19
Anno Domini	In the year of (our) Lord	
a..d.		
ante diem	Before the day (Nones, Ides)	
A..M.		38
Artium Magister	Master of Arts	
A.S.		38
Anno Salutis	In the year of (our) salvation	
A Ω		**5**
Alpha Omega	The first and the last (letters of the Greek alphabet)	
Cf.		
Confer	Compare	
D.D.D.		**44**
Dono Dedit Dedicavit	Gave and dedicated as a gift	
D.N.I.C		**21**
Dominus Noster Iesus Christus	Our Lord Jesus Christ	
H.M.		**48**
Hoc monumentum	This monument	
H.S.E.		**5**
Hic Sepultus Est	Here is buried	
i.e.		
id est	That is	
I.H.S.		36
Iesus Hominum Salvator	Jesus the Saviour of men	
LL.D.		**1**
Legum Doctor	Doctor of Laws	

Abbreviation	Latin	English	Page
M.D.	Medicinae Doctor	Doctor of Medicine	42
M.P.	Monumentum Posuit	Placed (this) monument	35
M.S.	Memoriae Sacrum	Sacred to the memory	4
P.C.	Poni Curavit	Caused to be placed	
P.M.	Piae Memoriae	To the pious memory	48
q.v.	quod vide	Which see	
R.I.P	Requiescat in Pace	May he rest in peace	6
R.S.S	Regiae Societatis Socius	Fellow of the Royal Society	
S.M.	Sacrum Memoriae	Sacred to the memory	6
S.S	Sanctae	Saints, Holy	31
S.T.B.	Sanctae Theologiae Baccalaureus	Bachelor of (Holy) Theology	
S.T.P	Sanctae Theologiae Professor	Professor of (Holy) Theology	30
X R	Chi Rho	The first two letters of the Greek name of Christ	5
1^{mae}	Primae	First	33
2^{dae}	Secundae	Second	33

2°		**3**
Secundo	On the second	
3^{tio}		**43**
Tertio	On the third	
7mo		**22**
Septimo	On the seventh	

Some Names

Andreas, Andreae	Andrew
Bercheria	Berkshire
Cornub(ia)	Cornwall
Cantabrigia	Cambridge
Cantuaria	Canterbury
Carolus, -i	Charles
Eboracum	York
Eduardus, -i	Edward
Etonia	Eton
Exon(ia)	Exeter
Gualterus, -i	Walter
Gulielmus, -i	William
Hantonia	Hampshire
Henricus, -i	Henry
Hugo, Hugonis	Hugh
Iacobus, -i	James
Iohannes, -is	John
Londinium	London
Mathias, Mathiae	Matthew
Oxon(ia)	Oxford
Ricardus, -i	Richard
Simo, Simonis	Simon
Vigornia	Worcester
Wintonia	Winchester